Hikers' Stories
from the
Appalachian Trail

STACKPOLE
BOOKS

Published by
STACKPOLE BOOKS
5067 Ritter Road
Mechanicsburg, PA 17055
www.stackpolebooks.com

10 9 8 7 6 5   3 2 1

Printed in the United States of America

Cover design by Tessa J. Sweigert
Cover photograph courtesy of Shutterstock

Cataloging-in-Publication data is on file with the Library of Congress

ISBN 978-0-8117-1283-5

Contents

CONTENTS v

The Final Stretch

Francis and Lisa Tapon   **Southbound**
Blood Mountain, GA
Monday, November 26

The AT doesn't let Northbounders off easy. After hiking 80% of the miles, they run into the toughest part, with the most treacherous weather.

That's one of the reasons we chose to head south on the AT; we knew that the hardest part was in Maine and New Hampshire. Sure, people warned us about Georgia, but we knew it was nothing compared to Maine.

In short, we thought we would get off easy.

We were wrong.

The weather forecast had predicted rain. Little did we know how much we would get.

After Jim Chester (a trail angel who let us stay at his house) dropped us off, we began to walk up and down the steep hills of North Carolina. The rain started coming down that afternoon. It rained while we set up camp, it rained hard that night, and it was raining when we woke up.

We had set up our GoLite tarp poorly, so a little bit of water had leaked in from the side. It wasn't a big deal because our synthetic bag keeps us warm even when we're wet.

Here's a simple fact: I don't care what method of rain protection you use, if it rains for more than 48 hours straight, you and your gear are bound to get wet.

That next day it rained all day long. Rain. Rain. Rain.

After slogging through the rain and mud, we came upon a solitary twisted old oak tree, which marks the famous Bly Gap, the northern border of Georgia! We knew we only had 76 miles to go, about three days.

We set up our tarp in the drizzle and drank from the cool piped spring nearby. The wind really started picking up that night. Fortunately, we were dry in our tarp—at least, as dry as we could be.

We awoke to the beating sound of the rain against our tarp. Tired and a bit moist, we crawled out into the rain, packed up, and moved on. Our obsession with Springer Mountain, the end of our journey, pushed us on.

That day, the third day of rain, was like a monsoon. Although we had experienced incessant rain in Costa Rica, this was truly impressive. Nature was letting us have it. The wind whipped so hard that it bent our strong GoLite umbrellas. They didn't break or get inverted, but they were certainly tested.

The constant rain made it hard to eat, since the rain would rarely stop for more than thirty minutes. In the end, we had to cross our fingers and cook a warm meal up when there was a slight letup in the rain. A couple of times we timed it poorly and were drizzled on while we were cooking and eating.

We pressed on.

That night, we stopped hiking at 6 P.M.—abnormally early for us. Mentally exhausted, we wanted a good night's sleep. The previous night we got slightly wet because it was raining so hard and we didn't set up our tarp very well. Normally we can get away with a sloppy setup, but when it's raining hard and windy, you must be meticulous.

Perhaps we were getting lazy with our tarp setups as we neared the end of our journey. Or perhaps it's simply because weren't tested enough in our journey; indeed, many AT historians pointed out that we received less rain than normal this summer.

This night, however, we didn't want to get wet. Therefore, we made our tarp a rocket ship.

Indeed, as Francis thrust the final stake into the ground, he couldn't help but admire his masterpiece: a whopping fourteen guy lines tied tightly to make the GoLite tarp look like a spaceship. It was low to the ground, and one side (Lisa's side) would be flush to the ground, to make it simply impossible for water to leak through. After admiring the aerodynamic shelter, we snuggled in for a good night sleep.

As we drifted asleep, Francis had visions that Al Capone and his cronies were standing outside the tarp, armed with machine guns. All night long the cankerous machine gun–like rattle of rain battered against our thin tarp. The last time we were pelted so hard by rain was in Maine.

The rapid-fire rain hammered our tarp all night, but we were safe in our spaceship. For twelve hours we lay huddled in our dry home as nature unleashed its fury upon our surroundings.

We cooked a warm meal under our tarp the next morning, while the rain continued to slam for the fourth day in a row. Although we ate freeze-dried food for two and grits for two (two full servings each), we were hungry just two hours later. That just goes to show that the expensive freeze dried meals don't supply a thru-hiker with enough energy.

Branches and trees had fallen all over the trail, making it a veritable obstacle course. After hiking until midday we pulled aside under a pathetic roof (a trailhead sign with a roof 2 feet wide). That was when M.A. (Maine Author), a section hiker, came by and offered us a ton of food. That trail magic was the beginning of our good fortune. By the time we put the last morsel of food in our mouths, the rain had stopped!

Even though the clouds lingered for a few hours, by late afternoon we felt the warmth of the sun's rays. What a glorious feeling!

To celebrate, we found a nice open space off the trail and unpacked everything we owned. After four days of incessant rain, everything was wet. And wetness means weight. Our packs felt about five pounds heavier than when everything was dry.

We lounged around and ate a satisfying meal. Meanwhile, all our gear and clothing was drying off quickly, thanks to GoLite's intelligent fabrics. We slapped our (once again) light packs on our backs and set off to Springer, with only two days to go.

We received our next-to-last trail magic from Dan, who drove us to Helen, Georgia, so we could enjoy being tourists in this German-like town. Then he took us into his home and gave us the shower and bed that we treasured so much. But nothing was as good as being able to do laundry after so many days in the rain! Thank you Dan!

Georgia was tough, but not because of the terrain. It was hard because of the weather conditions. We'd been hoping to waltz the final 150 miles into Springer, but the AT had other plans.

Nevertheless, once the rain stopped, we breezed over Blood Mountain, the tallest mountain in Georgia. Many Northbounders had warned us about it, but we almost didn't even notice it. Maybe that's because at Neels Gap, right before Blood Mountain, we were each given a free pint of Ben & Jerry's ice cream as our reward to making it within 33 miles of the end. We savored every bite with big, bright smiles across our faces. We gazed into the nearby horizon and saw Springer Mountain smiling back at us.

The Shakedown

Corwin Neuse (Major Chafage)   **Northbound**
Walasi-Yi Center, GA

I walked confidently into the outfitter at the Walasi-Yi Center, threw my pack upon the ground and issued the defiant challenge, "Shakedown this!" Then a clerk politely told me to quit blocking the aisle for the other customers, and that if I wanted to have a shakedown, I should make an appointment with one of the sales team. I meekly retrieved my pack and quietly did as told.

Things were rather hectic at the outfitter that morning. A clerk ushered me into a side room with two other hikers. We waited patiently for someone to attend to us, and watched with some unease as a janitor scrubbed the entrails from a previous shakedownee out of the carpet. Apparently they had been so ill-prepared for the hike that their brain had exploded in shock. It was quite messy. Still, I was confident I would not meet the same sticky fate. I knew what I was doing. I'd been backpacking before, after all. This wasn't my first rodeo, as the saying goes. Admittedly, it was ten years earlier, and had only lasted for eleven days, and I don't remember having to carry a tent or wearing more than one set of clothes. But I still had that experience to fall back on. I was going to be fine.

A gruff, mustachioed man came in wearing a skirt. Whenever a man wears a skirt, you know he means business. One with crazy facial hair, who stinks slightly of gunpowder and gin at nine o'clock in the morning, even more so. Cursing impatiently under his breath, he instructed us to empty our packs out on the floor, and then to stand in the corner, pull our pants down and grab our ankles, because it was about to get ugly.

"Empty your packs out so we can get started," he said. "I'm going to go assist another customer, but I'll be back when you're done."

Slightly wary of his aggressive instructions, I began to unpack. I couldn't help but compare myself to the other two. They were brothers, part of the Foot Clan, as they called themselves, probably because they realized they all had feet. One was named Stinky Foot, the other was named Furry Foot. Or something. Whatever their names were, I couldn't help but feel like I was better off than them. They were both carrying musical instruments, guitars or possibly banjos. Please.

The man in the skirt returned. We all snapped to attention.

"Okay, let's see," he said, surveying our equipment. "Y'all have backpacks, that's the first step. If you don't have a backpack, and you try to hike the Appalachian Trail? You're gonna die."

Good, I have a backpack, I'm not going to die, I thought.

"Next thing you gonna need is a twenty degree sleeping bag, or better. If ya try to get through the Smokies with a sleeping bag that's less than twenty degrees, y'all are gonna die."

I held up my EMS 20° sleeping bag. Check. He nodded.

Athlete's Foot or whatever he was called held up his sleeping bag. A 32° Eureka bag. Oh no.

"Oh no," said the man in the skirt. "See, that's not going to work. I know that says it's thirty two degrees, but it's really more like forty. Maybe even fifty. Now I know lots of y'all think you can just go to Walmart and buy any old bleep, and you might be fine. But if you try to hike through the Smokies with that, you're gonna bleeping die."

The man had a kind of a salty vocabulary. I was so impressed, I felt a cascade of urine spraying down my leg.

"All right, y'all got stoves? You got cook pots? Whatchu doin' with that big ol' thing?"

He was talking to me. I looked down at my 1.6 L cook pot. It was too big?

"Oh, someone's joining me," I said, "On the trail. Later. Maybe."

I thought my sister might join me on the trail when her job let out at the end of May. The man in the skirt nodded.

"You got your boots. Good. You got your socks. Good. No, you got too many." He was talking to me again. "You only need three pair. Put the others aside."

Indignant, I put aside my other sixteen pairs of socks. Why would anyone try to deprive a man of his socks? It just seemed inhuman.

"Why do I—" I started to ask, but he shook his head, cutting me off.

"You're gonna die," he said, by way of explanation.

I knew he was right, and looked down at the floor, ashamed.

"Now, thermals? Check the tag. Are they any percent cotton?"

Mine were 5% cotton. So what?

"Mine are 5% cotton. So what?" I said.

"If you try to hike anywhere with cotton clothing that's even a little bit cottony, you gonna die."

There was no refuting that logic.

I ended up sending home most of my socks, along with my journal, which I hadn't written in, a pair of sneakers, my winter jacket, which wasn't waterproof, and my thermals. It was rather painful.

"Now, don't you worry, we'll fix you up nice and good," said the man in the skirt, now ignoring the Foot Clan entirely. They sat in the corner, sobbing quietly over their banjos. The man in the skirt continued, ushering me into a different area of the store, "Now, I got these here Patagonia thermal bottoms, made out of unicorn hair. They weigh negative thirty pounds, they're fireproof, and I can get them to ya for the special price of $3,000."

He looked at me eagerly. I admit, I was a little hesitant. His smile faltered.

"Plus!" he said, "I can give you my personal guarantee that if you buy these, you ain't gonna die!"

"I'll take them," I said, immediately regretting my decision.

"Now, rain gear. This here jacket is made out of Mythril. By the dwarves! It's good to negative a thousand degrees, and—"

I had to cut him off. "I'm sorry, sir. Mythril? Don't you have anything in Adamantium or Dragon Scale?"

I left the Walasi-Yi Center about half an hour later, eight pounds and $250 lighter, but also secure in the knowledge that at least I wasn't gonna die.

The Meltdown

Nicole Green   **Northbound**
Walasi-Yi Inn, GA
December 28, 2010

Trekking the first 30 miles, we've met quite a few Southbounders (SOBOs) who are near to finishing their journey. Our conversations with them remind me constantly that the trail is not just one thing; it is many things to many people.

For us, this section of the trail is a beginning, but for them it's the end. One section may be a wicked mountain ascent for me and a jolly day hike down a hill for someone else.

Around six days into our actual hiking we met a newlywed couple called Ragamuffin and Mega Mo. They had some advice to pass on to us:

> *Never decide to leave the trail in town or on a bad day.*
> *You will have bad days.*
> *You will cry.*
> *It will get better.*

These words were especially helpful to me, since three days into our hike, I had a major meltdown. One mountain after another broke my spirit and wore me down until I finally fell down in tears crying, "I can't do this. I hate this. I want to go home."

A lot of people don't talk about those experiences, but many have them. Something like fifty percent of people who try to thu-hike don't make it out of Georgia. It's not that those fifty percent couldn't do it and the other fifty percent could. It's that the second fifty percent chose to keep going.

7

The things that kept me going were the following: Pete, my family, and you, the readers of my blog.

Pete was very mad when I said I wanted to stop. Understandably. I was leaving not just the trail, but him, too. He came with me to town and asked me to at least sleep on my decision. I agreed.

All I wanted was to go home and spend the holidays with my family. I justified that I could leave, spend the holidays at home, and come back later when it would be warmer and "easier."

But I knew in my heart that if I left, I'd probably never come back. And I knew my family would rather I keep working at this goal, despite how much they missed me.

At the time, I'd just started to write regularly and get feedback from readers. I hated the idea of letting them down by giving up.

After a restless night, I realized that if I left then, I would have lost. I would have done with this trip exactly what I've done with the rest of my life, skated through on the path of least resistance.

I told Pete that I would commit to getting at least to Helen, where our first food drop was supposed to be. (Only 50 miles into our 2,178 mile trip.)

We've hiked four days since we left that hotel, and despite cold weather with a still insufficient sleeping bag and an Achilles heel injury that has us taking yet more zero-mile days, I have been happier on the trail than I could have imagined. Following that rule of not giving up on a bad day reminds you that there are more good days than bad and gives you just enough extra energy to make it to the next summit.

Then, as you keep hiking, each summit becomes a reward in itself.

I may not end up finishing the whole trail; we'll see. I want to, but what I know I will do is follow the guidelines. I am committed to trying to get out of Georgia. I will not stop on a bad day. I will continue to challenge myself to do even more than I ever thought possible. I will hike as long as I choose to, but if I stop it won't be because "I can't." It will be because I make a choice.

As it stands, this trail has strengthened me already, and I see why people continue to come back over and over again.

Snow, Slush, Ice, Mud, and FUN!

Amanda Redpath (Veggie)   **Northbound**
Hiawassee, GA
March 9, 2010

Dude: Howdy

Me: Hey

Dude: If you see a dog with a collar, let people know, I lost one of them.

Me: Well, you have seven more, how many people are you dog walking for?

Dude: I'm hoooog huntin'.

Me: How do you hog hunt? I didn't know there were hogs up here.

Dude: They ain't supposed ta be. That's awhy I'm huntin 'em. [Something I couldn't understand in thick southern accent.] Weeell, ya let the dawgs out 'n they bay 'em, then I shoot 'em.

Me: Uh huh, have a good day now.

Well, it has been an interesting ten-ish days now and we are in Hiawassee. Georgia, almost to the North Carolina border. We started out going up the approach trail after eating as much fresh fruit and mate as I could fit in my stomach on March 1st. It was just about one of those rare, perfect hiking days with no mud and a bright blue sky; the temperature was around 60 degrees with a slight breeze.

We stayed in Springer shelter that night. During the night, we got hit with a blizzard. The prediction: 1 to 3 inches. Reality: 6 to 10 with some fun 3-foot drifts. I had a BLAST. It was just like hiking in the Adirondacks, but in Georgia. As I watched everyone freak out in the morning, I just snuggled back into my sleeping back until the wind died down enough to make breakfast. The next few 10-degreeish nights were a hell of a lot of fun in a 20-degree sleeping bag.

Mom didn't seem to enjoy the snow as much as I did, as I made some snow creatures, wrote messages with my hiking poles, and constantly measured the depth. Apparently, many people went off the trail quite quickly because this amount of snow is not normal in Georgia. Whatever, I still had fun. Although the second day, I did burst out laughing because I didn't think karma could get you a year and a half later. I was walking until this branch/bush thing and my pack nudged it sending a large lump of snow on my head. All I could think about was when that happened to Jeremy and I laughed my ass off. Ha. Ok.

The past four days, the temperature has been in the 50s and 60s and awesome, but all the snow has not melted. There are some large icy chucks on the sides of mountains and some slick slush mud mix.

In a conversation with dad…

Me: Hey dad, guess what?

Dad: What?

Me: Remember when we did that 7 mile "rim trail" on the Grand Canyon and we were having fun running around and mom was freaking out?

Dad: Yeah, of course, we had to chase your hat.

Me: Mom still freaks out on the sides of mountains or things that drop off.

Dad: (Laughs) That so now?

Other than that, we are meeting some characters, including a dude with a large Coleman stove and 4 pounds of bacon named Kentucky and another with frozen blue jeans named Cotton. Enough said there. Oh, and the many others.

Right now I have to go check to switch my laundry because I'm writing this with a towel wrapped around my waist and my checkered scarf around the top. They are my new "laundry clothes." Pictures will not be on the internet.

Peace and happy trails!

One Last State

John Pugh (Johnny Swank)　　　　　　　　**Southbound**
Hiawassee, Georgia
Jan 7, 2001

I'm sitting in a Laundromat in Hiawassee, Georgia, making a laughingly vain attempt to get the funk out of my clothes. Having not seen a washing machine in more than a week, all my clothes, not to mention myself, were in dire need of a thorough cleaning.

I don't know much about Hiawassee other than: It's located in north Georgia; the entire town seemingly shuts down on Sundays; and, most importantly, it's about 67 miles from Springer Mountain and the end of my journey.

The weather the past few days has been beautiful, with highs at times reaching 40 degrees. I knew my sense of temperature was gone when, on seeing my thermometer read 25 degrees the other morning, I was thinking, "Today's going to be a scorcher."

One thing this trip has taught me is that everything is just a matter of perspective and attitude. If I can feel my fingers and toes, then everything's cool. (God, that's a horrible pun, but again, I'm just going to roll with it.)

Right now I'm wearing my last pair of semi-clean but very dark socks. My theory is that they'll act as little heat sinks on my feet, soaking up and storing all those blessed BTUs for the coming days. Only time will tell how much this dubious plan will work.

Another thing I've learned out here on the tundra of the AT is the awesome power of man's ability to reset and adapt to the harshness of his environment. Case in point: One night a few weeks ago, a few hikers and I were talking about the sometimes gruesome reality of having to leave the relative warmth of your sleeping bag to go to the bathroom (Bathroom? How about the woods?) in the middle of the night.

The only way I can describe this most horrible event is that it is analogous to going back through the birth process again, leaving the warmth and security of your sleeping bag to go out into the shockingly cold, cruel world. Indeed, when it's 5 degrees outside and the wind is howling, it is truly like getting a smack on the butt. Many, many nights I've stayed in my bag for what seemed like hours in self-denial that my bladder was the size of a basketball, yet unable to will myself out of my sleeping bag. "Should I stay or should I go now?" I think, "If I stay, there's no way I'll be able to sleep, even while gritting my teeth until I have a headache. If I go, I will surely freeze." I bounced around a few ideas.

- Stop drinking water—no bathroom needed. Upside: Get to stay in sleeping bag. Downside: Death by dehydration.
- Get fitted with catheter and associated ankle bag. Upside: Get to stay in bag. Downside: Line to bag may freeze, causing blockage and severe discomfort; unbalanced walking from only having a bladder bag on one ankle.
- Purchase one extra water bottle. Urinate in bottle as necessary at night. Upside: Get to stay in bag. Downside: Emptying bottle in morning; mistaking said bottle for drinking water in middle of night, leading to foul breath or worse.

I met two hearty souls yesterday at a shelter. They had started their own thruhikes heading northbound on New Year's Day. I gave them such scholarly, sage advice as, "Dude, don't sweat this hike. Just take your time and be flexible." Also, "Hey man, you've got to get off the trail and hit the all-you-can-eat buffet at the Shoney's in Franklin. It rocks."

It's interesting to see some folks going through the same doubts, questions, and considerations at the beginning of their journeys as I did. This whole trip has been one long learning experience, not only about the nuts and bolts of functioning on the trail, but more importantly and more valuable, about myself. For me, the journey on "the trail between the ears" has been as meaningful, if not more so, as the trail itself.

I finally crossed my last state border into Georgia yesterday. It wasn't much of a crossing, just a small sign tacked to a tree near Bly Gap. No brass band. No fireworks. Regis Philbin wasn't even there to interview me. None of that was necessary, though. Just the rush of coming across that line after many months of effort was reward enough. I hope I didn't wake any bears with my hollering.

Honestly, it did feel great. I sort of visualized in my mind that I might be sort of bummed out at this signal that the trip was coming closer to finality, but that hasn't come to pass. Like all things, this journey too must come to an end, at least in the physical sense.

Emotionally, I almost feel the journey is just beginning, like a huge door of possibilities I've always held within myself has just opened. It intrigues me to actually see and acknowledge that thought. As I've said, being out here has given me copious amounts of time to think, to feel, and to breathe in life and become much more aware of myself and my place in the universe.

The snow that once completely covered the hills is starting to recede a bit. Below 3,500 feet, I'm actually walking on bare ground for the most part. I've become much more aware of which side of the mountain the trail crosses. On the side with a southern exposure, much of the snow and ice has almost completely melted away, while the more northerly exposures have seen little change. This makes it a little difficult to estimate how long a given mile will take to cover, but most of the time the more conservative time is accurate.

My worst-case scenario puts me at the end of the trail about 4 or 5 days from now. I almost cringe to even say that, but if this little stretch of warmer weather holds, everything should work out fine. Or as a buddy of mine I've met out here (Compañero) and I say, "No matter what happens, it's going to work out."

The rain that was forecasted has come in with a vengeance. It should clear out by tomorrow afternoon, though. All this rain will either:

• Help melt some more of the snow off, making hiking easier.
• Freeze solid at night, resulting in me doing a 65-mile ice skating race à la Eric Heiden.

The only certainty is that I will be very, very damp for the next couple of days. Wet possibly, but damp certainly.

This section of trail is blessed with several outstanding views. In particular, the summits at Wayah Bald, Albert Mountain, and Standing Indian Mountain were spectacular. My favorite, though, was probably from the observation tower at Wesser Bald. In and of itself, the view was impressive, but I happened to hike across the top just at sunset to the most remarkable display of colors I've seen in a long, long time. The deep reds, vibrant oranges, and many shades of purple came together in an intense mixture that seemed to shimmer and melt into each other. Very cool. Very cool indeed.

I took several photographs, but a picture can't capture that perfect moment in time. After watching the sun go down, I still had five miles to cover. These miles seemed to fly by. The temperature started to fall in its familiar pattern. The wind stayed calm, so much so that every footstep in snow magnified in intensity. I could feel the beating of my heart, my lungs filing with air, and every part of my body felt so incredibly alive.

Hiking late in the day like that often brings me such moments. Dawn and dusk have been my favorite times of the day to hike, although the prospect of leaving my sleeping bag before the sun comes up doesn't seem likely to happen again anytime soon.

Well, the laundry's done and so am I. I just about smell April fresh for the moment. One advantage of being out here when it's cold is that the cold keeps the funk down. Mind you—not all funk is bad funk. George Clinton sees to that, but James Brown got there first

Anyway, I'm going to hike to the Mexican restaurant in town now and pound down something like 100,000 calories, if I can. Sounds like a plan.

I'll Be Your Personal Cheerleader

Nicole Green   **Northbound**
Franklin, NC
February 6, 2011

Those of you reading my blog regularly know that I've had a few strug-gles on this trip. I've questioned my ability to do this and needed a whole lot of encouragement from Pete to keep going. It feels good, for once, to be writing a blog about the other side of the situation.

After our eight-day stay in Franklin, Pete and I trudged back up the mountain to pick up where we'd had to get off. I hate getting off the moun-tain for weather, because it usually means backtracking, road walking, and logging a lot of non-AT miles onto our feet. The days we spend hiking that include no white blazes (the marks that designate the Appalachian Trail) are really frustrating for me.

So when we arrived back at the Standing Indian Shelter for the second time, I expected to simply set up camp, eat a quick dinner as usual, and rack out for the night. Upon arriving, though, we found that we weren't alone in the shelter (this is unusual for us, winter hiking). Walking up to the three-sided log building, we were met by the faces of two rather dejected-looking men. They'd just started a fire and plopped down in front of it with very little enthusiasm or energy.

They were up for an annual guys-only weeklong hiking trip, but hadn't expected their first day to include breaking trail in over a foot of snow. They'd spent a zero day in the shelter and were planning on leaving to go home the next day.

Over the course of the night, we four sat around the fire, sharing stories, songs, food, and beverage. Luckily, the power that a campfire seems to posses worked its magic. As the night grew darker the guys cheered up and began to laugh and tell stories about other trips they'd taken. The crackle and pop of wet logs accented the lighter mood and served as a symbol for our ability to brave the cold of winter hiking. If they çan make a fire from frozen logs, I told them, what's a little snow while they walk?

I shared my story. I shared the humiliation of breaking down in tears three days in and calling a shuttle to take me off the mountain and into town so I could go home. We all shared stories of sore, wet feet and cold nights and waking up to frost around the mouth of your sleeping bag.

Slowly, the guys began to realize that there's always a bad day in most hikes and that the fun of making miles and sitting around a fire and waking up to the most beautiful sunrise you've ever seen make it worth the snow and cold and soreness.

The next morning, as we all packed up and prepared to part ways, they thanked me for being their personal cheerleader and credited me for keeping them on the trail. I was just glad to pay forward the gift that someone else gave to me.

Child's Play

Second Stage (Elaine Rockett) **Northbound**
Nantahala Outdoor Center, NC
Feburary 21, 2010

Winter came down to our home one night
Quietly pirouetting in on silvery-toed slippers of snow,
And we, we were children once again.
—Bill Morgan, Jr.

I awoke early at Cold Spring Shelter to the musical burble of the water flowing just feet away from the shelter and the first rosy glow of dawn. A leisurely stretch in the sleeping bag loosened my muscles without exposing me to the chill air. What a pleasant way to start the day!

The night had been quiet, and no bear had disturbed my food, which was hanging on a mouse trapeze in the shelter. I usually don't keep the food with me, but my failure at hanging the food last night had left me with an unusually shortened bear bag line.

The Nantahala Outdoor Center (and a shower!) was on my mind, so after coffee and a quick breakfast I packed up as quickly as I could and set off. The trail took me out past the bear cable that had proved so frustrating last night. The snarled ends of my bear bag line laughed down at me. On such a beautiful morning I couldn't help but smile back.

The trail wound up and over Copper Ridge Bald. It was still early on the frosty ridge—perfect for a couple of photographs. The early morning light slanted across the landscape below, highlighting the ridges that marched away into the distance. Such beautiful country!

17

There were some blowdowns and snow on the trail, but it wasn't nearly as physically demanding as the previous day had been. The only tricky spot was a blowdown right at a switchback. I tried to limbo my way under, lost my footing, fell, and slid downhill until a tangle of branches grabbed me. Lying on my back (on the entangled backpack), I had to free myself from the snare of smaller branches and flip over, turtlelike, to get my legs under myself—and avoid hitting my head on the main trunk of the downed tree above or slipping on the snow. It must have looked like a solo game of Outdoor Twister, Challenge Edition.

When I got to Tellico Gap I noticed a dramatic difference between the north-facing slope I had just descended and the south-facing slope I was about to ascend. The one was still covered in snow and ice, and the other was free of the nasty white stuff—a welcome sight, to be sure.

I hiked up the trail a bit until I found a friendly rock. It was dry, sunny spot. There I had a pack-off break, basking in the sunshine. Lunch was a full affair with food spread out before me on the rock, instead of a power bar of some sort eaten while standing in the snow. What a treat! What a change! It did my spirits good. That was more like it!

I didn't relax too long, but continued up to Wesser Bald. The yells of what sounded like a group of guys engaged in rough horseplay came from direction of the fire tower there. I decided not to investigate but rather head down the other side. Suddenly I was facing icy snow again with a some-what steep, but wide, descent. It was obvious that plenty of people had been up here, perhaps over the weekend, as there was a depression down the center of the path where feet had packed the snow down. Evidently it had been warm enough to melt some of the snow, and then cold enough to refreeze the snowmelt as the trail was very smooth and icy.

I tried to babystep my way down, bracing myself with my hiking poles. My feet did not sink in at all, but slipped and slid as I inched my way down. All of my muscles were tense, anticipating a slip and then a fall. I was afraid I would simply slide all the way down to the bottom.

It was very slow going, but then the idea hit me. *Don't fight it; join it!*

I sat down in the track, tucked my hiking poles into my armpits like a downhill skier. Gravity and the slickness of my rain pants did the rest.

Soon I was speeding down the slope. Leaning to the side and shifting my weight allowed me to take the turns in the trail without stopping. When the slope lessened to the point that I slowed too much, I would lean for-ward, tip the poles down, and then lean back hard against them. That would give me enough push forward that I continued sledding downhill— although I didn't think of it as sledding. I considered it to be a new AT Winter Olympic event: the "luge-ski."

I went on for quite a ways in this fashion. Soon I was whooping and laughing like a wild thing. All too soon it was over and I lay back on my pack and giggled. After a couple of minutes of lying on the cold snow, I wiped the tears from my eyes and struggled to get up. With the pack on, my first attempts did not work. So I rolled over and off of the trail. I got my arms under me and thrust down hard with my hands to push myself up—only to find my arms elbow-deep in the unpacked snow and my nose and glasses coated with white. This made me laugh all the more. Finally I managed to get to my feet and sedately walked down the trail—but with a huge grin on my face. I felt so much like a kid.

Hurrying on, I was aware of the miles left to reach the NOC. The trail undulated along, up and down, up and down. Everything was fine until I reached "the Jump-off."

I don't like slippery footing. I don't like narrow places. I don't like heights, and I don't like drop-offs in the trail.

This place had them all.

I managed the first turn okay. But then it got icier. I tried to walk down, but couldn't find a way that felt anything like safe. Eventually I sat down and tried to inch my way down. Unfortunately, the same slickness of the rain paints that had contributed to the fun on Wesser threatened to send me headlong—uh, leglong—off the narrow ledges there. At one point I did start sliding and ended up with one leg dangling over the seemingly bottomless abyss. I tried to scooch back up the trail but couldn't find any purchase. I tried to roll over, but the movement triggered a subtle but definite drift toward the already too-close edge. No matter what I did I seemed to slip closer and closer to the edge. I couldn't control it.

Before long I was whimpering like a baby, "No, no, no." This was an "I want my mommy," kind of whimpering. If there had been a button to beam me home, I would have used it, even if it had meant never seeing the AT again. I was terrified.

Eventually I unbuckled my pack, wormed out of its straps and tried to lower it to the trail where it switchbacked below me. I lowered the pack as far as I could then let go. It fell the last few feet and rolled. And rolled. And rolled. In slow motion it rolled up over the curb of snow at the edge and started to topple over the little crest, about to fall into the great chasm, when it was snagged by a rhododendron and balanced just on the edge. It looked as though a breath of wind would be enough to send it crashing below.

I manoeuvred myself down to the pack. But the trail was still too narrow for me to be happy. The ice and snow was too slick for me to stand up and put my pack on, as scared as I was.

I sat in the snow for a long time, feeling too shaken to go on. Finally I put the pack in front of me, held onto a strap (that I could let go of if it threatened to pull me off a ledge), and did the butt-scoot all the way down until the trail widened out enough to where I felt confident enough to stand up, put my pack on, and continue like a real, grown-up hiker.

For those who have not seen this section, know that countless hikers do this stretch and probably give very little thought to it. Without the ice and snow, even I would have been okay, if a bit nervous, picking my way down. My fears made it much worse than it really was, I'm sure. Nevertheless, it was completely unnerving for me.

I was shaking and scared and ashamed. I found that in the slipping, sliding, unorthodox descent I had lost the bite valve and bite valve cover from my water bladder as well as my confidence and sense of humor. The day had gone from beautiful, exciting, and amusing to gray, threatening, and unpleasant in a very short time.

The Trail and the idea of making it to Maine no longer entered my mind. All I was focused on now was to get *down* out of these mountains and out of this snow, as soon as possible.

Fortunately, I had no trouble on the descent to the NOC—just a long slog as evening fell. The walk would have seemed easy and pleasant but for the sense of defeat at having been so badly shaken over what should have been simply a few difficult minutes.

When I got down to the river, I found that the entire collection of buildings that makes up the NOC campus was locked up tight. I wandered around looking for signs of life. Eventually I found my way to "Base Camp," a collection of basic bunkhouses and a community building. There were some men taking a Wilderness First Responders class who were staying at the bunkroom, but they had no idea of how I could check in. In the end, I found an unlocked bunkroom and let myself in. I showered and then heated some dinner in the community kitchen. I had some pleasant conversation with the students and then retreated to my bunkroom, where the day caught up to me.

With the Jump-off incident on my mind, I felt subdued and disheartened. The shaking fear had left me but had been replaced with a sense of failure. I realized that, while I *could* have fallen, I hadn't. I was unharmed and could continue my hike. However, I felt like such a child, such a baby, that I wondered if I really have what it takes to complete a thru hike.

I gave trail angels Sherpa Dave and Robin a call to let them know I was in safely and gave an account of the day, as well as my fears and doubts. Soon Robin had me laughing, the incident was put into a more realistic perspective, and I felt much better.

Maybe I'll be able to make it after all.

Southern Generosity

John Bryant Baker (Sunshine)   **Northbound**
Sassafras Gap, NC
April 4, 2010

It is a crisp, clear Easter morning as we make our way towards US HWY 19 and the Nantahala Outdoor Center. We are looking forward to getting our resupply and spending an afternoon by the Nantahala River. The steep decent from Wesser Bald and "the jumpoff," as the guidebook described it, have left my knee aching, swollen, and in need of a break. As the few buildings that comprise the N.O.C. come into view, they are accompanied by the rustling yet peaceful sound of the river. The first building we come upon is the Wesser General Store, so we decide to take a look and see what they have in stock. In addition to getting enough food to get ourselves to Fontana Dam where we have a mail drop awaiting us, we are hoping to find a phone card. Lola and I had decided to deactivate both of our cell phones for the first part of the hike, but with it being Easter Sunday, we thought it would be nice to call our parents.

As we walk the few aisles of the store, the clerk, Hank, introduces himself and asks us if we are thru-hiking. He's spent a lot of time on the trail and says he loves this time of year when the hikers start coming through.

"Let me know if you got any questions or needed anything," he offers. I do not seen any phone cards, so I approach the front counter in order to ask. "Nah, don't carry any phone cards. Used to, but with cell phones and all, people don't seem to have much need for 'em anymore. There's a gas station 'bout a mile up the road. You could check there."

Disapointed, I say thanks. Neither of us have any desire to walk an extra two miles for the mere chance of finding a phone card.

Hank quickly stands up from his seat, sensing our disappointment and realizing the needed to further explain what he had already assumed we should do. "Nah, nah, I don't mean walk. Take my truck."

I am utterly confused and caught off guard; my forehead immediately wrinkles and my eyebrows furrow as I lean in ever so slightly closer to Hank. Surely I must have misheard, I think to myself, but he continues.

"You got a driver's license?" Yes, I nod. "You know how to drive a stick?" I nod yes again. "Well hell, take my truck. The keys are in it. You can leave yer packs right there underneath that table."

I clumsily slide my pack under the table, still completely disheveled. My brain is having such a hard time processing what just happened it has seemingly cut off signals to my extremities and any dexterity thereof. Did this total stranger just offer us his truck? I was not sure if he is crazier for offering or if we are crazier for accepting. As we make our way out the front door, still unsure if this is really happening, Hank motions to his white Chevy S10 and loving adds, "Just be gentle when puttin' her into first. She can be a little tricky."

I press down on the clutch and turn the key in the ignition. Had I been blindfolded, I would have thought I had started a monster truck. The engine roars, the muffler backfires, and the entire truck shakes like a dog at the front door ready to go for a walk. Lola and I look at each other and cannot help but smile from ear to ear.

We make it up to the gas station, the truck roaring and backfiring the entire way. We pick up a few things, but never are able to find any phone cards.

As we get back in the truck, I fire her up and am about to head back down the road to Hank and the Wesser General Store when I notice a man slowly walking on the sidewalk in front of us. As he walks by, he never stops looking at me, and he is grinning, like he knows something that I do not. He makes his way past the front of the truck and then stops, raises his hand to wave, and yells over the sound of the muffler, "Hank let you borrow his truck, huh?" I smile, wave, and nod in agreement. We are not the first hikers to experience Hank's generosity, and I am sure we will not be the last.

Welcome Back, Friend, You've Come a Long Way

Peter J. Barr (Whippersnap)   **Northbound**
Russell Field, TN
April 7, 2010

Most people at the shelter this morning got an early start. 3 Bears and I opted for a relaxing morning and took our time, enjoying our last access to a bathroom, running water, and trash cans. We set out together and crossed Fontana Dam. This was yet another place I had driven so many times and wondered if I would ever be crossing it as a thru-hiker. I had a feeling today might turn out to be an emotional day and it was. We walked the road up to the start of the foot trail up to Shuckstack.

I quickly set a brisk pace and left 3 Bears behind within a few minutes. This mountain and section of trail once beat me and a friend up, and I was eager to show it that I was back. I was also eager to get to Shuckstack.

I didn't stop once going up the mountain. My breathing was heavy but my emotions heavier. Several times I began tearing up and would cry while walking.

Nearly six years ago, my friend Brad Davis and I set out from Fontana Dam to traverse the Smokies on the AT. We knew nothing about hiking or backpacking. We had rented old gear and set out in our tennis shoes and cotton shirts, with a big chip on our shoulder. How hard could it be? We would find out quickly.

Brad is one of my best friends. I asked him to take that trip with me and despite his busy schedule at his summer job, he made things work and went with me. I would never have gone had he not come with me.

We crossed the dam and could see the fire tower looming on a summit high above, as I could see it today. We were so excited. Today I passed a spot on the trail that I remembered where Brad told me that he would do anything to help me out, like accompany me on this trip. I passed spots where I remember both of us huffing and puffing, bent over gasping for breath even though it had been less than a mile. I passed spots all day today on the trail where we deliberated turning around and calling off the trip because it was just too difficult. Later, on our first day, I lied to Brad and told him we would call for a ride and bailout at Newfound Gap, just past halfway. I never intended for us to do that, but it made him continue. I suspect he won't mind after all this time.

During today's initial ascent I could see the tower getting closer though the trees. I sped up. The skies were mostly clear. My good fortune has stretched so far—after sun and blue skies the entire way though the Nantahalas, I still get a near-perfect day to visit the most special place to me on the whole trail.

I thought back to making this hike with Allison on a hot Fourth of July. I also thought back to just last October when I climbed to Shuckstack with the National Park Service's archaeologist and landscape architect to campaign for the tower's restoration and discuss its future.

The final pitch up to the summit is infamously steep. The last several times I climbed it were without a heavy pack. But I still did not stop until I reached the base of the tower. I climbed it quickly—not one stair at time in a sitting position like I did six years ago when Brad and I reached this point. The tower shook even more violently now, the stairs wobbled worse, and the sounds of creaks were much louder after several more years of neglect and deterioration.

Once on top, I began sobbing. I sent Brad a message thanking him for making that trip with me and telling him that it changed my life. It was here six years ago that I looked out across the high Great Smoky Mountains and fell in love. It was this view that made me determined to finish that trip. It was this view that began my fascination with fire towers. It was with this view that I fell in love with the mountains, the outdoors, and western North Carolina. Climbing this tower for the first time altered the direction of my life. Me visiting it again on my Appalachian Trail thru-hike was all of these events coming full circle, a culmination of my time that I have so significantly dedicated to the mountains since that first visit.

Until I climb Katahdin, I doubt there will be a more emotional moment for me than my visit to Shuckstack today. While I started at Springer Mountain about two weeks ago, the journey really started right here, six years ago. That day, the mountains entered into my blood and have never left—nor do I think they ever will leave.

Shuckstack has its own fascinating history. It was erected in 1937 by the PWA, nearly a decade before the existence of Fontana Dam. When construction on Fontana Dam was initiated, the tower and its watchmen of the period had a bird's-eye view of the work, which went on 24 hours a day for 3 years. When it was complete, the flooding of the Little Tennessee River was observed from the tower. The subsequent creation of the 35-mile-long Fontana Lake was perhaps western North Carolina's most dramatic landscape change ever and it was visible from the Shuckstack tower.

Reaching the fire tower today was like visiting an old friend who has fallen on hard times. It felt as if the tower remembered my first visit like it was yesterday. It spoke to me and I spoke to it. I told it "I'm back"; it replied, "Welcome back, friend, you've come a long way." It wasn't talking about the trail. As I left I looked up at it and told it I would be back and that I promised to help it. As I walked away it said, "I know. I'll see you soon, friend."

The rest of today's hike was relatively easy. I was once again in prime hiker form, firing on all cylinders. My blisters were mostly healed, my Achilles tendon much more flexible, and my muscles and lungs as strong as ever. I attribute all of this to entering the Great Smoky Mountains National Park today and coming home to the mountains. Nowhere else in the mountains have I spent so much time, explored so thoroughly, given so much, and received so much back than in the Smokies. I've hiked all their trails, climbed most of their peaks, quested for their secrets, and even celebrated marriage in the Smokies. While everyone else is just passing though, I'm home again. Everything is familiar and memories pour over my mind with nearly every turn of the trail.

I unceremoniously reached my third state of my journey today. There is no sign to announce it, but I hit the North Carolina/ Tennessee border on the shoulder of Doe Knob. I made a 100-yard side trip to the summit, as I am now passively collecting 4,000-foot peaks. I later side-tripped all 20 yards to the top of Devils Tater Patch just beyond Mollies Ridge Shelter. I noticed significant evidence of rooting in the soil by wild hogs on both summits, and on the side of the trail throughout most of today. I hope to see one while I am in the park, though I hope more to see a bear. Though if I do not, I can't be overly disappointed—I've had the good fortune of seeing 30 bears in the Smokies alone in the last six years.

I also passed through Ekaneetlee Gap today. Nearly everyone hikes though here unaware of its history. But this low dip in the western Smokies crest is one of the most, if not *the* most, historically significant gaps in the entire range. Here an ancient Indian path crossed the Smokies. This path was a crossing from North Carolina in the Eagle Creek drainage to Cades Cove in Tennessee. The Smokies' main divide remained largely uncrossed and unexplored even into the 1800s. In fact, when William Davenport surveyed the entire Smokies crest, becoming the first person to ever walk this high wild divide, he noted only two trails crossing the crest, one at Ekaneetlee Gap and the other in the vicinity of Dry Sluice or False Gap. For hundred of years Indians and later settlers crossed at this gap. In the future, I'd like to retrace this now off-trail route.

I had intended to stay at Mollies Ridge shelter tonight. This is where I spent my first night in the Smokies, first night in a shelter, and first night on the AT. When I reached the shelter I went in and lay in the bunk where I slept that first night. That night I was naïve enough to take a Snickers bar to bed with me and put it next to me as I slept. Within five minutes it got entirely pulled into a crack in the stone wall by a mouse, frightening me and keeping me up much of the night.

At Mollies Ridge I rested in the cooking area built onto the side of the shelter. I envisioned Brad and me six years prior, foolishly attempting to assemble our rented cook stove. It was at this shelter I first met Rowboat, a thru-hiker I followed for the rest of his journey to Maine in 2004.

Today at this shelter I met Ox, a 1997 thru-hiker who is a passionate trail maintainer in the Smokies for the Smoky Mountain Hiking Club. Since moving to Knoxville, Tennessee, two years ago, he has preformed maintenance on nearly every trail in the park and logged hundreds and hundreds of volunteer hours. I thanked him repeatedly, as I was endlessly appreciative of his work and dedication and that of all the other trail maintainers. I have been astonished with the impeccable condition of the trail thus far all the way from Georgia. I had been so worried about blowdowns caused by the harsh southeastern winter but they have thus far not been an issue, thanks to the work of people like Ox.

Ox was also a Smokies 900 completer, and even a South Beyond 6,000 completer, to my delight. I persuaded him to work on the Lookout Tower Challenge next. We had a lot to talk about and we chatted for an hour at Mollies Ridge (and would talk for another hour at the next shelter this evening). He is a passionate hiker and a true asset to the Smokies—a good guy in my book.

I reached Mollies Ridge relatively early and was still feeling strong, so I overcame the sentimental urge to remain at Mollies in the name of progress and friends. I could knock out another 2.5 miles by pressing on— and 3 Bears, Bryant, and Lola had recently done so, and I wanted to continue to enjoy their company.

The trail to Russell Field was a pleasant walk. Much relocation had extended the distance but lessened the grades. I made the shelter in under an hour. I found the shelter empty with the exception of 3 Bears, who was napping on the top bunk. Ox dropped by for more good conversation before heading down into Tennessee and home for the night.

Just 3 Bears and I tonight in the shelter, much to our surprise. It is nice being able to spread out all our gear. This is the last AT shelter in the Smokies with the bear fence on the front. We're closed up safe from the bears but I suspect not the mice.

We are both hoping to make Newfound Gap by Friday night to get down into Gatlinburg. A big thunderstorm is due tomorrow. Our good run of about 10 days with no rain is finally up. I am rather concerned about hiking on the high exposed ridges in the storm. It may prove my biggest test thus far of this hike. I will be all wet and won't reach town for another day. It is supposed to get very cold, too—into the 30s. Ironically, we go over Thunderhead Mountain tomorrow!

Don't Stick Your Nose Where It Doesn't Belong

Amanda Schlenker
(writing for Hansel and Gretel)   **Northbound**
Cherry Gap Shelter, TN
April 15, 2011

It is AT terms time again!

White Blaze: Following the "official" Appalachian Trail as marked from start to finish (what Hansel and Gretel are doing).

Blue Blaze: Hiking parts of the official AT but also taking some side trails, short cuts, or alternate routes.

Pink Blaze: Hiking the trail in the romantic pursuit of the cute girl ahead of you.

Ladies and gentlemen, Gretel officially has a pink blazer! (But honestly, who could blame the guy? She's a good catch!) This pink blazer fellow does have a known name, but for this story, we will just refer to him as "Pinky." Hansel and Gretel met Pinky a few days ago. He followed them into the town of Erwin, Tennessee, (340 miles from their start at Springer Mountain) and then followed them out. He stuck with them for a few days, all the while making passes at Gretel, who dodged him time after time while slipping in "my boyfriend" at every opportunity.

One day on the trail, Gretel arrived at the designated break spot in the middle of the day. Hansel was already there and snacking along with a group of male hikers (Pinky included) who made Gretel feel "uncomfortable as a woman," so she blazed through without stopping. It wasn't long before Gretel heard someone hiking behind her, undoubtably Pinky. She started running to keep distance between her and him until she came to a stream.

Now the #1 rule of thru-hiking is to take care of your feet and keep them dry. Wet feet lead to all kinds of discomfort—blisters and more. Any body of water should be handled with care, and any other day, Gretel would have taken her sweet time to cross this stream. However, today her only thought was to move as quickly as possible.

You can guess where this is going. In no time flat, Gretel slipped and fell in the stream, soaking her shoes and socks all the way through, with Pinky right on her tail. As she scrambled to get out of the stream she realized that not only did she have soggy feet, she also had managed to fall so that a thin stick shot its way right up her nose!

"I didn't know you could get anything that far up there . . . I was seriously gushing blood," she said, and it seems Pinky saw it all. But strong-willed Gretel was still completely set on avoiding any and all contact with this dude. She refused to stop, blood or no blood, and forged ahead, wiping her nose frantically as she walked. Pinky called after her, offering his concern, his help, a Band-Aid, but Gretel wanted none of it.

"I'm fine!" she yelled back. He asked her if she was bleeding, but she was so flustered that she couldn't think of anything to tell him except, "A stick went up my nose." She tilted her head back and kept on trekking. Pinky kept on her tail and Gretel continued to reject his help. When they reached a flat spot in the trail he charged ahead of her, accusing her of being a P.I.T.A. (Pain In The A**).

Glad to have finally shaken Pinky, Gretel continued to the shelter in her own happy, bloody, soggy solitude. She reached the shelter with a massive headache to find Hansel waiting for her, grinning from ear to ear.

"What did you say to that guy?" he wanted to know. Apparently, Pinky had angrily told Hansel that Gretel was the most stubborn person and continued onward.

At least Gretel had successfully rid herself of her first Pink Blazer. It's just too bad her nose didn't fare better.

The moral of the story: Don't run from Pink Blazers. We have not yet identified a preferred approach, but if you run, you will surely end up with a stick in your nose.

Happy trails!

To the Max

Peter J. Barr (Whippersnap)   **Northbound**
Max Patch, NC
April 14, 2010

"Nowhere else on the Appalachian Trail do I feel
so strong an urge to return."
—*Earl Shaffer, on the Smokies during his 1948 thru-hike.*

I had a big day. Perhaps my longest hiking day yet. With side trips, I put up a deuce deuce. My feet are suffering for it, though my body remained strong throughout the day. Today was like a southern Appalachian highlight reel. I had great views from a fire tower, and two 4,000-foot grassy balds.

I awoke to discover that I had bested the resident lookout tower mouse. He had not gotten to my food, which I had hung from one of the metal rafters in the tower. I had observed where he entered the tower cab and plugged the mouse hole as well. I slept quite well. What a great spot to spend the night! It was like my own personal clubhouse that a kid dreams about. Perhaps this is a root for my fascination with the job of tower watchman.

The sunrise from Mt. Cammerer was a dramatic way to begin the day. A fitting end to my time in the Smokies as the sun illuminated its high peaks for me one last time. Last night I enjoyed the dazzling spectacle of city lights lining the valley as I looked down upon Newport and, distantly, Pigeon Forge. This morning I watched a helicopter swoop between peaks as it entered the Pigeon River Gorge. It was probably a thousand feet above ground, yet I was looking down on it at least two thousand feet below me.

I got a somewhat late start for the big day I had planned. It was hard to leave White Rock, hard to leave the tower, and especially hard to leave the Smokies. My first 0.6 miles didn't even count, because they just took me back to the AT. Shortly into the descent is one of my favorite trail construction features on the whole AT—a CCC-built S-curving stone wall lining the outside of the trail as it winds its way through the rocky outcrops on a ridge descending from Mt. Cammerer. Earl Shaffer took a photo of this trail and rock wall when he passed through in 1948. Apparently we both found it aesthetically pleasing and appreciated the workmanship. And it is yet another piece of the AT that has remained unchanged in its route since its beginning in the 1930s, which I like very much since I get to literally walk in the footsteps of my heroes and all those to make the journey over the years. There are too few original sections like this remaining. The CCC sure did a good job in the eastern Smokies, as the trail here has largely, if not entirely, remained unchanged. At the wall I took a cell phone photo on the rock outcropping overlooking the Big Creek Valley. This is the place where Allison took the picture years ago that would become the author photo used in my book and press releases.

As I descended the main crest of the Smokies, I entered into spring for the first time. While I had been reveling in spring temperatures for a while now, this was the first time I came into a forest where the floor was entirely covered in green and many of the trees had newly budded leaves. It was very exciting to see life returning to the mountains.

I remember descending this section with Brad in 2004. It wasn't funny then, but it is now: Brad was claiming he surely had suffered permanent damage to his knees, which were aching so badly he could barely walk. Luckily, he walks limp-free today, yet ironically he makes fun of me for my five percent–disabled classification in my left shoulder that the insurance company bestowed upon me following its initial injury.

I stopped at Davenport Gap Shelter for water. I knew with the monster climb ahead I had better start forcing hydration or water loading in advance of the climb. I collected four liters and I drank at least two and a half before the climb up Snowbird. Soon I reached Davenport Gap, where Brad and I ended our 2004 inaugural hike. We were dismayed to learn we had another two miles to walk to our parked car. Brad's "permanently damaged" knees didn't like that . . .

This spot was also where William Davenport concluded his 1821 survey of the Smokies crest—the first person to ever make such a journey, especially pre–trail era, and probably the last to do so until Harvey Broome, Carlos Campbell, and company did it in 1931. A traverse of the

Smokies range, especially the eastern Smokies, during the wild, untrailed days has always been most fascinating to me. Now that I think of it, Arnold Guyot surely completed a Smokies traverse himself in the 1950s, though I am uncertain if it was all in a single trip.

For whatever reason, Davenport decided that the Smokies ended at this gap and not about two miles further at the more logical Pigeon River. So adamant was he that the Smokies concluded here, he carved a stone and dated it to mark the end of his survey. The stone is still there today, though up the hill and in the woods, missed or ignored by most. The date, 1821, is still very legible, though I have a suspicion its etching was enhanced in the 1930s when the NPS reset the stone in concrete. It is a fabulous historical marker denoting the successful end of an amazing, wild journey by a brave man. And now my own journey in the Smokies was coming to an end here. How greatly I enjoyed my time here, and how dearly I will miss them! But I will be back, for they are my home.

The Carolina Mountain Club maintains the next section of the trail north of the Smokies. I thoroughly enjoyed the section between Davenport Gap and the Pigeon River, much of which travels parallel to State Line Branch, with several scenic cascades.

I crossed the Pigeon River on a highway bridge. This section of the trail is most unfortunate, especially the first quarter mile that ascends the concrete pavement of the I-40 exit ramp before crossing under the interstate. I wish there were a long, pedestrian-only suspension bridge over the river just for hikers, as there was slightly upriver near Waterville when Earl and Gene came through. The astounding continuity of the trail is severely broken here, for the first time since the start. I dearly hope this will be fixed in the future, but know that it will never be a high enough priority.

Nevertheless, crossing under I-40 was significant for me. Countless times I had driven the highway into Tennessee en route to a Smokies hike. Never once on my way did I fail to look down and see the white blazes crossing under the bridge and reentering the forest and never once did have I failed to imagine myself someday passing through on a thru-hike. Today was that day.

While a better choice than over the Smokies, it is most unfortunate that I-40 had to be cut through the gorge. My hiking friends and I often discuss what a wild and dramatic place the Pigeon River Gorge would be without an interstate and if it was part of the National Park. The Nantahala Gorge would look puny in comparison. Today and in the future we still suffer the consequences of building this highway through such rugged terrain. A landslide in October has had the interstate through the gorge closed for months, including still today. It was odd passing under it with no rushing traffic overhead. It should have been like this all along, though even I can't come up with a more reasonable western passage for American travel and commerce. After all, this is better than Indian Gap, where everyone crossed into Tennessee prior to the 20th century.

I opted not to visit Standing Bear Hostel. This was a sacrifice I had to make based on my desire to reach Hot Springs by Thursday night. But I have stayed there before and have enjoyed speaking with Curtis in the past. Last time, in 2008, I gave him a copy of my book.

I snacked and got more water before the dreaded climb up Snowbird Mountain. On Green Corner Road, Southern caught up with me, slightly irritated that I had not arrived at Davenport Gap Shelter the previous night as I had declared my intentions of doing the previous morning. This deceit was necessary to secure my solo perch in the lookout tower. While I would have enjoyed Sothern's company, I could not risk telling even one person; it could ultimately have had a result as if I had told twenty people. I did feel somewhat bad, as I really like Southern. He is about my age and reminds me so much of my college roommate, Mark, that I feel we have been friends for years already.

The climb up Snowbird Mountain was long, hot, and hellacious. As if a 2,500 foot climb out of the Pigeon River Gorge wasn't already difficult enough in the intense heat, the trail was absolutely decimated with blowdowns. It was a nightmare obstacle course. And every fallen tree across the trail was always too high to go over yet too low to go under and usually too thick to even straddle. While I didn't enjoy the climb, I still made good time and didn't need to stop the entire ascent. My body can now readily handle long, arduous climbs quite well, even if my mind still struggles in advance and during them.

I reached the summit of Snowbird Mountain and to my surprise and utter delight discovered the peak was a grassy bald with fantastic views of surrounding mountains, especially the Smokies to the west. I had expected the funky white FAA tower at the summit, but not these exciting, expansive views. The climb was utterly miserable and I was drenched in sweat and my clothing and pack straps had all turned almost completely white from salt. Yet the view made it worth it, especially because of the surprise. Mt. Cammerer looked strikingly pointed from this perspective, perhaps having more face prominence from this angle than any other. It looked like a tall spire, and it was particularly satisfying to know that I had camped on top of it last night and had walked all the way here from it in only hours. I felt the same way when I viewed Mt. Guyot, its tall triangular peak looming large in the background. I had hiked off-trail to climb it just two days ago and a view of it from this point made me pleased that I did.

I could see the bald summit of Max Patch to the east. It was my destination tonight, still 10 miles away. I had hoped to make it there for sunset, but knew I would need to maintain high pace to achieve that goal.

I did achieve it, thanks to hard hiking. Much of those 10 miles were without views so I remained focused on walking, though I took a snack and water break at Deep Gap and another short stop at Brown Gap to address a blister problem. I had discovered the culprit causing my newest blister—an old band-aid that had remained in my sock had been stuck under a toe and rubbing it.

The final few miles to Max Patch were literally like trying to reach the end of a rainbow. If you have ever sought out that pot of gold, you know that the rainbow just keeps getting farther away. Max Patch was my pot of gold. Though the final climbs were not severe, I was convinced that I would reach Max Patch after cresting a series of consecutive knobs. After about five, I decided it absolutely had to be behind the next knob. To my dismay, another knob presented itself, and Max Patch curiously now seemed farther away than it had two peaks prior. It was endlessly frustrating, though this phenomenon seems to have a way of presenting itself at day's end, especially after long hikes like today's.

I finally reached the western North Carolina gem that is Max Patch, and yes, it's entirely in the Tar Heel state. We may share the Smokies with Tennessee, but the claim to Max Patch is ours alone. And what a claim it is! An expansive, broad, entirely grassy bald mountain. It truly is a spectacle after emerging from hours, or rather days, entirely in the wooded forest.

I once camped on its summit with Allison, and visited it again on a short hike with my groomsmen prior to my wedding in 2008. Walking to it, rather than driving, made it significantly more rewarding. This is the first true grassy bald on the AT. Its rolling green slopes extended down to gaps on all sides, unlike on Snowbird Mountain and several balds in the Nanta-halas, which have a clear patch only at the summit. It was exhilarating climbing to the summit—a half mile of hiking with constant views in all directions. It was difficult to focus on walking rather than looking.

I finally reached the top and with at least a half hour to spare before sunset, which allowed me to set up camp. I spoke at length with a charming couple honeymooning in Hot Springs. They had hiked up to enjoy the sunset. They were my age and reminded me greatly of Allison and me. I was also very proud that they chose western North Carolina as their destination for their honeymoon. It certainly is worthy of such an occasion, and tonight's display on Max Patch was excellent. I gave them my card and I hope that they leave me a note on my website in the future. Seeing them enjoy the mountains together made me especially eager to see Allison.

I use a great amount of adjectives and hyperboles to describe the sunrises and sunsets which I have been so grossly spoiled with during my adventure thus far. I must say, that while all have been stunning, tonight's display on Max Patch may have been the best of all. It was certainly my favorite sunset thus far. The distant mountain ridges turned innumerable shades of blue as the sun declined above them. Both the setting and the scene were surreal.

Now the stars are out in all their glory. What a special place is Max Patch! I intend to return here frequently for as long as I am able. From sunrise to sunset, today has been a particularly memorable day on the Appalachian Trail.

English Muffin

Stuart Skinner (Tintin)   **Northbound**
Roan Mountain, TN
April 18, 2010

I'm done feeling sorry for myself and have let go of the anger I felt at the raucous hikers at Uncle Johnny's who kept most of the people at the hostel up. I've got no problem with people drinking, I just get a little pissed off when they choose to get bladdered and talk bollocks all night right next to your tent. But I've decided to take more control over my trail experience and not let it be dictated by the behaviour of others.

It may seem somewhat hypocritical to rant about hikers drinking, then choose to go off to a bar a couple of days later, but I'm not just out in the U.S. to hike the trail; I'm here for the cultural experience too, and to sample small-time America. The offer of free pizza and $2 beer at the Beer Wash, a local drinking hole in Roan, seemed like a good opportunity to hang out with some locals.

I didn't want to advertise the fact that we were going to the other hikers. That may be selfish, but I didn't want it a bunch of hikers to descend upon the place in their droves and take over the bar. Thin Mint decided to stay at the hostel, as free pizza and $2 beer was too enticing to literally walk away from. Creepy rocked up just before we set off, and Buzz . . . well, Buzz went to the bar, bought two cases of beer, brought them back, and drank most of them, knowing he was going back to the bar. Buzz is a short, rotund farmer from Georgia. He's not a man of many words and those that he does speak are in said in such a thick Southern drawl that he might as well be speaking Dutch.

36

The Beer Wash is about as a classy as its name. The bar walls are coolers lined with cases and cans of beer, with only a small area to sit in. We made our way out back and Hunter and I decided to play some darts, a game that I love going to the pub to play with my mates back home. There were a couple of pool tables with some old boys who could shoot pool all right, yet couldn't seem to stand up straight, swaggering as they approached the table. Country and western music was blazing out of the jukebox, Coors Light was flowing, the air was thick with smoke, and there were women with cowboy hats; I couldn't have asked for a more authentic experience.

I wanted to play one of the locals at pool and try to strike up conversation in the process. I approached one man, dressed in camouflage gear, which I have found out is considered fashionable by some folk out here, a pony tail, and a baseball cap sporting the Confederate flag. I made my way over and sheepishly asked if I could play the winner. "I don't care," he said and he clearly didn't. All eyes were on me and there were smiles as Hunter and Co. found my attempts to make friends amusing.

"You don't want to play with them. They're mean," said Buzz flatly, eyeballing them up. They weren't the friendliest folk, I'll give him that, but they didn't seem mean, just not very receptive to strangers.

Buzz went over to the next table, where a man of smart attire was playing against one of the cowgirls, whose face was as leathery as the boots she was wearing. Buzz seemed to pride himself on his ability to connect with fellow, small-town folk from the south. It worked. It was game on—Buzz and I versus the pool sharks, Beth-Anne and Hank. They had their own pool cues, so it was serious business. We'd only played a few shots each before Buzz disappeared.

"Where's your buddy gone?" asked Hank.

I had no idea. With all the beer he'd been drinking, I assumed he'd gone to relieve himself. "I think he's gone to the bathroom," I offered.

Now Hank looked at me all funny. It's the quizzical, slightly confused look I get when it registers with the person I'm speaking to that I'm really not from these parts. "The bathroom," mimicked Hank.

I quickly corrected myself. "Sorry, I meant restroom." I wanted to mingle, not stand out, which is kind of hard when I look like a tramp yet speak with a very middle-class English accent.

"Now where you from?" asked Hank. I was interested to see what his reaction would be when I told him, yet slightly nervous, as I didn't want too much of a scene.

I may not have wanted a scene, but it was quite the scene that followed when I told him I was from England. "ENG-LAND!" he shouted. "Well heck, ain't you kind of cute," said Hank as he approached me to shake my hand. I was mistaken. He didn't accept my handshake but instead put his arm round me and squeezed me in tight. Oh dear. "You can be my English muffin."

I really didn't want him to be my American pie and I began to get very nervous, uncomfortably so when he asked me if I liked men. I may have been out in the woods for a while, but not even Leatherface appeared attractive to me even with her cleavage practically spilling over the pool table when she went to take a shot. I felt very awkward and wanted him to let go of me, yet I wanted to remain friendly and not offend the man.

"You ever seen *Deliverance*?" he asked. I had seen the film of the canoeists terrorized by Appalachian rednecks that included the notoriously disturbing scene where one of the characters gets raped whilst being made to squeal like a pig. It was obvious that Hank was doing his very best to make me feel uncomfortable. He was succeeding all right. "You know I'm just fucking with you."

I looked up and old leatherface was cackling away. "Don't worry honey, he's just messin' with ya'll." Well, he messed with me all right and even though I knew he was joking, there was some part of me that wasn't entirely sure, and I was relieved when he let go of me.

Buzz returned, armed with a load more beer and we continued playing—well, I played whilst Buzz swayed. I got my revenge on Hank by cleaning up whilst they had four balls remaining, even with Hank pinching my bum just before I played the black, trying to put me off. *That'll show you,* I thought. Buzz came up to me and told me quietly that I was meant to let the locals win. Sod that. I want to take as many locals down at various games as I make my way up the U.S. National pride is at stake each time I play and I want them to remember the time they got beat by a Limey at their own game.

It was a successful night out. We all had a great time, laughed a lot, and met some interesting characters. Buzz and Hunter were offered the opportunity to get to know one of them a little more intimately. There was an old "cougar" at the bar, which I've been told is an older single lady who hangs out at bars in hopes of luring younger men back to her place. Kind of like a MILF only she wants to F you and not the other way round. This cougar wasn't content with just one, wanting to take both Hunter and Buzz back home. Hunter wasn't interested, but Buzz certainly was. I think we did him a favour by coaxing him back to the hostel. Maybe we did her a favour, but it was almost one in the morning and we have a 24.4 mile slack-pack planned tomorrow. This English muffin needs to rest a while!

What a Ride!

Stuart Skinner (Tintin)   **Northbound**
Dennis Cove, TN
April 20, 2010

Last night was perhaps the most terrified I've been on the trail. I was awoken at four in the morning to the sound of something crashing down the hill, branches snapping, trees falling. Well, that's what it sounded like. It was making its way down the hill, heading straight for my tent. I was certain they'd find my half-eaten remains the next day, as I was far away from the hostel. I panicked, not knowing what to do. Despite my stance on guns, I wanted one, a real big one. Big enough to take out armoured vehicles. Alas, all I had to fend for myself was noise and I let out an almighty "Woooooooo!" as though I was welcoming my favourite band on to stage. Pretty pitiful. I rushed to grab my head torch, quickly unzipped my tent, and poked my head out, expecting to lose it in one foul swipe.

I had no idea what I'd do if I saw a bear staring at me in the face. I'd probably go into cardiac arrest and so it wouldn't matter. I wouldn't do anything because I would lack the ability to do so. Every time I go scuba diving I pray I'll see some big sharks. They fascinate me and I am obsessed with them. I want to see a bear, too, but when I'm awake and on the trail, not whilst I'm all alone in the dark. I guess I'm not scared of sharks because I know a lot about them. I don't know much about bears, only the terrifying tales of them, which is probably why I have an irrational fear of them. I just associate all bears with grizzlies. I wouldn't have been surprised to see a Tyrannosaurus staring me in the face with the amount of noise that was made as something descended upon my tent through the woods.

For the second time in the space of a day, I had been fooled into fear by the calamitous crashing of a castaway, droopy-drawed dog.

Despite the best efforts of the folks at Kincora to shoo him away, it would seem that Rumplestiltskin sniffed out my scent and was doing his best to get into my tent. I felt bad for him, as it was raining out, but at the same time he'd scared the living daylights out of me and sleep became an impossibility, as I was pumped with adrenaline. It was hard to get mad at the loveable, lost eejit of a dog, though, and we made a compromise; he wasn't allowed in the tent, but I allowed him to seek cover in the vestibule. He didn't follow me to the hostel when I got up for breakfast; instead, he hurled himself off on into the bush, nose to the ground. I still had no idea what he was doing out here.

All the crowd at the hostel had planned a nine-mile slackpack. It hardly seemed worth it, but it was being taken in the spirit of an outing rather than a hike from one place to another. I can't blag my way out out of this one, as I went packless, only bringing a cup with me. There were plenty of water sources to be had and they lent to the serenity of the hike. We passed countless streams and rivers, and the beautiful Laurel Fork Falls. We passed one pool of water that looked like a great swimming hole. I love water and in all honesty, I'm more beach bum than mountain man. My friend Lloyd christened me "Duck Boy" on our bike trip, as I'd throw myself in any vestibule of water that I could find without hesitancy. I had to; it was bloody hot the whole time and needed to regulate my body heat somehow. I didn't need to cool down today; it was cool enough and I knew the water would be bitterly cold. I was going to walk on by, but I wanted to go into the water. The only reason I wouldn't would be that it was too cold and that's no excuse at all, especially after my resolution to be in control of my trail experience.

I want to hike without regret and throw myself into as many new experiences as possible and I decided to to take a literal approach to that. I stripped off down to my boxers and braved the waters. Pixie, Megladon, and Chef went from hovering around the water to following suit. I may as well have dived into the bloody Arctic, it was that cold, and I let out a "woooo!"—part shock and part excitement at the spontaneity of my actions. Pixie followed, then Megladon; then Chef and Three Bears turned up and jumped in too. The look on everyone's faces as they resurfaced, having plunged into the pool, was priceless. The water was shockingly cold and no one stayed in too long.

The water was invigorating and I felt alive. I had read a sign in a diner the other day that read: "Life should NOT be a journey to the grave with the intention of arriving safely in an attractive and well-preserved body, but rather to slide in sideways, body thoroughly used up, totally worn out and screaming 'WOO HOO, what a ride!'" This is now my trail motto. Although I haven't read this before, the sentiment expressed has been the fabric that has woven the life I have lived in the past few years together. "Live," Nietzche said, "as though the day were here," and each day I'm here I want to try and do something unique. Something memorable or out of the ordinary. Today that manifested itself in splashing in the swimming hole. We were all giddy with joy afterwards and I felt a new bond with hikers that I'd only say hi to in passing.

I was happy to have such a turnaround in events and the communal dinner later that evening was in stark contrast to the *Animal House* antics at Uncle Johnny's. We ate a home-cooked dinner together, without alcohol, enjoying the pleasure of each other's company. We celebrated having come this far with a cake that Three Bears made with 412.6 written in icing on it.

A lot of people out here are fans of the film *Into the Wild*; some are out here because of it. It tells the tragic story of a young man, driven by a deep desire to forge an independent identity of himself. Inspired by Thoreau and Jack London, he wanted to fend for himself in isolation in Alaska, to "live deep and suck out all the marrow of life, to live so sturdily and Spartan-like" (Thoreau). Christopher McCandless, aka Alexander Supertramp, was in part driven by the anger he felt towards his parents and some of their actions, particularly the infidelity of his father that had lead to him being a bastard child, something he was unaware of till much later on his life and then only by accident. This was to have a huge impact on his sense of self. He set off to Alaska to forge a new identity, one that he was in control of, starting with a new name. Christopher was a wounded young man and I can't help but think that he wanted to be alone so that he'd be safe and free from any more hurting. He died alone, but not before realizing the poignant point that "happiness is only real when shared." It's why I believe communal living is essential for the health of both an individual and a society. We've lost that way of living and I believe we have suffered greatly as a result.

A community is created by a shared reference point. We talk about a community of hikers and that's because we share the same objective: to thru-hike to Maine. It's why there is no concept of "stranger" on the trail, unless they be day hikers or tourons. It's why everyone seemed to be glowing with joy and laughter reverberated round the table.

There is something magical about Kincora; it's a place that does not command respect, but nurtures it. I have not been to a better hostel in all my travels, anywhere in the world, than Kincora. Bob Peoples is perhaps the most genuine man I've met out here; he lives a life of service, not just with the donation-only hostel, but with the vital maintenance work he does on the trail too. I plan to go back and become a member of "Team Hardcore," something that he runs after Trail Days where he enlists hikers to volunteer their time to give back to the trail by "hardcore" trail maintenance, or by creating a new, more hiker-friendly section of trail. I intend to be part of that team. There's a lot to be grateful for out here and I don't think I could go back home and be right with myself if I didn't give back somehow. The trail didn't just appear, it was built and is continually maintained. I don't want to be one of those hikers who take that for granted with a sense of entitlement, as they're "thru-hikers," and hike with that arrogant, selfish sentiment.

I'm in with a good crowd at the moment and I hope it stays that way so that I can share my happiness with some like-minded individuals. I hope to have many more days and many more nights like this one.

Adventures in
Hampton

Amanda Schlenker
(writing for Hansel and Gretel)   **Northbound**
Hampton, TN
April 20, 2011

Hansel and Gretel's last resupply down in Tennessee happened to be Hampton. Their experience in this town began when they picked up an "awesome hitch" (meaning they hitchhiked into town) from a great guy named Dan who had a fantastic southern accent. Hansel and Gretel climbed into Dan's car and they took off down the road. They learned that Dan is a dairy farmer and raises cows. About five minutes into the drive, Dan pulled over and said in his heavy southern drawl,

"Aww darn. I'm bein' stupid. Y'all wanted to go to Hampton. That's the uther di-rection!"

A quick U-turn and they were back on track. Dan asked Hansel and Gretel where they were from and was shocked to learn that they had grown up in New Jersey. He was expecting at least some hint of a Jersey accent. He said,

"I mean, I *know* I speak hillbilly. Y'all got *no* accent!"

When they reached Hampton, Dan bid Hansel and Gretel goodbye. He gave them his card and asked if they would call him sometime with an update on how they were doing. He was even so kind as to ask if they needed any money. Hansel and Gretel assured him they had enough, thanked him for his kind help, and headed for the town McDonalds where they ate plenty of satisfying junk food.

Then news of an all-day breakfast place met Hansel and Gretel's ears and Theresa's Grill instantly became an essential destination. When they entered this dive of a building claiming to be Theresa's, the first thing they saw was an old woman, silently sitting in a folding chair, giving them the death stare.

"Ahhh, hi! Can we eat here?" They asked. Nothing. Just more staring. Not knowing what to do, Hansel and Gretel just stood there and waited while Folding Chair Lady drilled holes through their foreheads with her eyes. Finally, another woman came out from a back room.

"Y'all can eat. Sit down. What d'y'all want?" She said dryly. She tells them they can't have biscuits and gravy because they are out of biscuits and gravy—which was interesting because some other guy came into the restaurant five minutes later, ordered biscuits and gravy, and got biscuits and gravy, but let's not get hung up on biscuits and gravy. The entire menu, consisting of about five items, was written up on a whiteboard. They ordered their meal, and for only $10, they ended up with a giant breakfast . . . which, needless to say, did not include biscuits and gravy.

Hansel and Gretel thought they should visit the restroom before heading out, but it's possible that they might have been better off saving it for the woods. The toilet was basically a seat on top of a wooden platform. Not only was there no toilet paper, there wasn't even a place to put the TP if the bathroom had been fully equipped.

It seems like Hampton's bathing accommodations are universally lacking. Hansel and Gretel couldn't find an adequate shower and ended up bathing in the bathroom of a gas station. They both agreed that the best part of their Hampton day was going to Subway, buying sandwiches, putting them in their packs and then eating them for dinner once they got to their campsite. Soooo good!

Safe from the Storm

I made it to the 500-mile mark today! And I made it to the month of May! And the state of Virginia!

I almost went home.

It was a storm that I would have been afraid of in a house, let alone in my Tarptent. Late on April 27th, tornadoes devastated much of Alabama and other parts of the South, including southwestern Virginia. I had just completed my first 20-mile day, stopping about 13 miles from Damascus, VA, and about 10 miles from the TN/VA border.

My original plan had been to do 23 miles to Abingdon Shelter, leaving a short 10 miles downhill to Damascus on the 28th, my mom's birthday. I was excited to get into Virginia and be able to talk to my mom on her birthday. It was such a beautiful day, and as I hiked across a field near Shady Valley, TN, the sun illuminated the greenest grass I had seen in some time. Fleet Foxes was playing on my iPod and I was elated, so happy to be right there in that moment.

As the day went on I could tell a storm was brewing as I hiked along a ridge 5,000 feet up, but I had no idea how severe it was going to be. I decided to set up my tent about 3 miles from the shelter for a couple of reasons: 1) I was tired and hungry and my beef stroganoff Knorr sides sounded like Thanksgiving dinner; 2) It was late in the day and I knew the shelter would already be full, especially since there was a storm threatening; 3) The storm hadn't hit yet and it was still light, so I could get my tent up before it started raining and got dark. I started looking for the first flat ground I saw.

I ended up setting my tent up in a little gap, but still along a ridge. I could see for miles to my right and to my left—not an ideal place to be in a storm. It was already really windy and I put big rocks on all four of my stakes to make sure they stayed in the ground. As I climbed in my tent, it was starting to get dark and the storm still hadn't hit—would it just pass by?

Around 9 P.M. the lightning started. The sky was constantly lit, with an occasional surge of light the was so bright I thought lightning had struck 20 feet away. Thunder rolled continuously, leaving it impossible to distinguish just how far away the storm really was. I was just about getting to sleep when it started to rain, a constant downpour that seemed to be coming at an angle—terrible news for me and my Tarptent, because there's about a foot of mesh between the ground and the bottom of the sil-nylon. I cuddled up in my sleeping bag in the very center of my tent as the sides started to get wet. I kept checking to make sure water wasn't building up anywhere on top of my tent, that would weigh it down and make it more likely to collapse.

It rained for a couple of hours and around midnight it stopped. It was calm for a good 5 minutes. I gave a deep sigh of relief and tried to settle back in and relax.

And then the wind began.

The paper the next day said that an F3 tornado ripped through southwest Virginia, the biggest one the state had ever seen. Winds of 135 to 140 mph roared through homes and truck stops and flipped over eighteen-wheelers. I doubt I got the brunt of it up on that ridge, but those were some of the strongest winds I've ever felt. I didn't sleep a single second that night. I spent the entire night bracing the side of my tent against the brick wall of winds and pleading to anyone, someone, if there is a God, to make it stop. I started to realize that a tree could fall on me sometime during the night and every time I heard a tree brush up against another, or crack, or a big gust come through, I covered my head with my arms.

I made it through the night and the next day I hiked down to Damascus. The events of the night before seemed like a dream and the magnitude of what I had experienced hadn't hit me yet. I got to Damascus to find the power to out everywhere with only the distant buzz of generators. The town was empty and dark and I entered the only open restaurant—Quincy's—to a round of applause from hikers and locals. "Towns! You made it!"

I found out that people had died the night before. That only 7 miles away a town was leveled—completely destroyed. My phone was dead and the cell towers were down. I walked up a half mile to the Food City that was running off of emergency generators, hoping to be able to charge my phone—no luck. But a manager overheard me asking a cashier if I could charge my phone and let me charge up my phone out in his truck. It took an hour for me to charge up halfway and I called my mom to wish her a happy birthday. I got a call through, but the signal was horrible and we couldn't hear each other. I texted her instead, and I knew I had to cut right to the point. "A tornado hit last night and I'm ready to come home" is the text I sent out.

I was freaking out and I began to think that hiking this trail was not worth it anymore, not if I'd be put in those types of situations. That night I slept, or hardly at all, despite being completely exhausted, at a hostel called "The Place." I was in the strangest place, surrounded by hikers who hadn't experienced what I had, who were normal and excited to hit the trail.

My mom and my girlfriend Pauline drove up to see me the next day. I cannot believe how amazing they are, patiently driving up to see me, not to take me home but because they care. We went out to eat and talked a little bit about it, but for the most part we just hung out all day. I was torn. I felt like I didn't want to play the game anymore. I was frightened, but I knew I would regret coming home. They understood completely and encouraged me to make a decision for myself that I could feel good about. I hiked out of Damascus on the 29th around lunchtime in absolutely perfect weather. I was uneasy, but okay.

In the couple days since, I've tented both nights, just to get it out of the way. The first night was strange, but last night I slept wonderfully. I hiked up Mt. Rogers and through the Grayson Highlands, and it was incredible. I can't really put into words the emotions I felt as I walked through country-side like I had never seen before. It was like I was out west, in Montana or something. I saw a couple of wild ponies but they were skittish and wouldn't let me get close; the rest must have been hiding. I'm in Troutdale, VA, tonight and it's basically just this diner with internet access and really awesome burgers and milkshakes. I'm sleeping at a Baptist Church tonight and I hit the trail again early in the morning.

I survived the storm and I'm feeling less shaken up—better each day. It's good to have some perspective, to feel how precious life is, sometimes. I know that the tornado was a freak incident and that I probably won't experience something that bad again, but there will be other storms—I'll just make sure to be in a shelter next time and not beneath the thinnest bit of sil-nylon imaginable.

My Name Is Woody Farmer

Karelyn Kressler (Little Dipper)   Southbound
Damascus, VA
October 26, 2009

The story of Woody Farmer is surprisingly simple. I mean, we knew the man for less than a day. Still, it took us ten states to complete his story . . .

Part 1: It all began back in New Hampshire when I and four trail mates (Yeti, After Dark, Lost Rob, and Curse) reluctantly awoke to the scuffling of an early riser. His trail name was Dancing Bear. He explained that the "Dancing" portion was somewhat mockingly bestowed since his hiking style was not graceful, often saturated with "Texas Two-Steps." The "Bear" part was dead on. He had hiked into our already overflowing lean-to the day before, making for a total of nine bodies squeezed into a space built for six.

And so there we were, awake earlier than expected, in a smaller space than expected, and in a more foul mood than expected. But Dancing Bear's conversation was kind and he kept it simple, as it should be in the morning. He was animated and jovial. I liked him. And in his break-of-day-discourse I had discovered something to smile about. And so I did.

My grin caught Dancing Bear's attention and he pointed in my direction, "You have a pretty smile." I blushed and covered my mouth, flattered. "And whenever I meet a cute girl with a pretty smile I just have to invite her back to my cabin." Alarms went off in my head and we all shifted uneasily in our sleeping bags. Hmm . . .

Perhaps sensing the uneasiness, he quickly added, "Of course, your friends are welcome too," motioning to my trail mates. Instantly we relaxed and became excited. All of us . . . ? A cabin? Seriously? He went on to explain that, yes, he had a cabin near Damascus and that he had been looking for some kind thru-hikers to host.

I pulled out my journal and began to jot down specifics. "My real name is Woody—now don't laugh—Farmer," Dancing Bear said. He told us to give him a call when we got to Damascus and he would provide us with good food, and a hot tub to boot! But, he said, there was just one more thing . . . "If she doesn't come with you, the deal's off." I was okay with this.

Part 2: Three months, and 1000-some miles later, we arrived in Damascus. And by this time the original group of five that had met Mr. Farmer had been disbanded. Yeti and After Dark had left the trail up in New England. Lost Rob had sped on and was now about a week ahead. Curse, however, remembering Mr. Farmer's dealbreaker remark, had stuck with me.

The story of Woody Farmer had become epic. We told and retold it to every thru-hiker we met, and each time I added better adjectives. I was nervous before I called him. What if I had gotten the number wrong? What if he didn't remember me or had changed his mind? I called, and perhaps he didn't remember me at first, but when I mentioned the phrase "thru-hiker," I knew we were in.

We had a lot on our plate the day we met up with Woody. We chose to "slackpack" (hike without our packs) 25 miles, and to do it all before the late afternoon rain. We were carrying a few snacks, water bottles, and that was it. It began raining before noon—a cold, persistent rain. I shook with the cold and mumbled through my words, but both Curse and "Skiman," another hiker we had met up with, helped keep me warm the best they could.

With limited cell phone reception, attempts to have Woody pick us up at earlier road crossings were foiled. All we could do was hike. We were hungry, and needed to stop for a break, but stopping meant getting colder. That's the way it is out here.

Finally, we made it to the road and quickly retreated to a nearby hostel to get warm while we waited. Woody was there in no time. He took us to get some groceries and we went to his "cabin" . . . ahem, MANSION.

His house is jaw-dropping gorgeous. He used the recycled wood from three other cabins to build his very own super-duper cabin. It had everything—sauna, hot tub, huge porches, high ceilings, modern conveniences like heat and running water, and more modern conveniences like air conditioning, TV, and an in-sink garbage disposal.

Woody escorted us into his home and into our hands he thrust bathing suits and bathrobes. He wrapped my robe around me and made me feel regal. Then he poured us heaping glasses of hot tea and told us to make ourselves comfortable. We downed the warm liquid and chatted, getting to know each other.

Eventually he told us to "grab a shower"—a request we were used to as thru-hikers. However, our showers were not to be in this cabin, but in one of our very own. Woody had built his cabin with a kitchen house (traditionally, richer families built the kitchen away from the main house in case of a fire). Woody's "kitchen house" had not only a small kitchen, but also a loft with twin beds, a living room, and a bath. It was just as beautiful as the main house, and it was all ours. The previous coldness of the day was soon forgotten.

We showered and thoroughly explored our new home. Then we rushed back to Woody's house and cooked dinner. It felt so good to cook again. I had missed all the spices.

We spent the rest of the night in the hot tub, chatting about our lives and loves, and watching Roy Orbison. Then we tucked ourselves beneath cozy quilts and fell asleep.

Woody had to leave early the next morning, but he wanted us to take our time. So, he put a house key on a string and lopped it around my neck. "Enjoy yourselves," he said. And so we did.

From the first smile to the last, I thank you, Woody Farmer. Your generosity and trust is hard to match. I don't know many who would do what you did for people they had known less than a day. Thank you for enriching my experience.

The Hills Are Alive

Second Stage (Elaine Rockett)   **Northbound**
Thomas Knob Shelter, VA
April 6, 2010

> *"There's music in the sighing of a reed;*
> *There's music in the gushing of a rill;*
> *There's music in all things, if men had ears:*
> *Their earth is but an echo of the spheres."*
> —Don Juan, *Lord Byron*

Tom, the shuttle driver, met me across from Mount Rogers Outfitters to take me back up to Summit Cut, where I had hiked from on Sunday. He saw my blisters and made some useful suggestions on how I might improve the situation. Unfortunately, there were no stores open that might have what I needed, so I put those ideas on hold until I got someplace I could get supplied. But now I wanted to hike! The couple of zero days in Damascus had me itching to get back on the trail.

Tom drove me back up the twisty roads to pick up my journey north. The early morning sun slanted across the road and flickered rapidly as we drove through the pattern of light and shadow. I started to feel a bit queasy, so I closed my eyes. Even with my eyes closed I could sense the rumblestrips of light jarring my head. Finally we were there, and I opened my eyes.

I hopped out, grabbed my pack, and headed north along the trail. It crossed some streams and headed up across some pastureland, then up again into the woods. A goat watched me as I climbed. When I got close enough, I tried to get a picture, but it turned out as so many wildlife shots do—"There, see that blurry white smudge there in the shadows? That's a goat!" It got nervous as I tried to slowly edge in for a better shot, and then it disappeared in a mad scramble over the rocks.

The day was warming up, and the climb went on and on. The early spring sun was beating down, and though I worried about sunburn, I had to change to a short-sleeved T-shirt to stay cool enough. My feet insisted that I slow down and pace myself even though the rest of me felt fine.

I came to a wide open area with a large rock—Buzzard Rock. It was hot and breezy, and the valleys were hazy and indistinct. I took a few pictures and moved onward and upward.

It was lunchtime when I reached the crossing of the AT at Whitetop Mountain Road. A small patch of shade under some trees provided relief from the noontime sun. I discovered that I was not alone in seeking shelter; ragged remnants of snowdrifts lurked in the coolness. My sweaty boots and socks dried in the sunshine while I had lunch and a short nap.

Another couple of miles found me at Elk Garden, an open grassy area where elk once lived. While the shade of an information board drew me in for another break, two small groups of spring-breakers drove in to walk for a short ways on the famed Appalachian Trail. They climbed the first hill, looked around briefly, and then returned to their cars and drove off.

No cars or people were visible as I put my pack back on, crossed the road, and resumed my walk. This part of the trail seemed open and desolate. One could easily imagine a herd of elk grazing on the hillside.

The trail left the open fields and entered the coolness of a forest, climbing and climbing. Water from many small streams and seeps flowed across the trail. Snow higher up must have been melting in the hot sun. The soft music of gurgling, tinkling, and splashing seemed to echo all around me, while from the ground at my feet I could only hear the squishing and sucking sounds of the mud pulling at my boots.

The trail turned rocky, with many roots running through and over the rocks. A stand of fir trees gave off an incredible aroma. It wasn't the evergreen scent of Christmas, making one think of cinnamon and candle wax with traditional music in the background. No, this reminded me of blue skies, a breeze whispering in the branches, the trickle of water, and a deep earthy smell—since that's exactly what there was.

Eventually the trail emerged from the trees not far below the summit of Mt. Rodgers and then curved away toward Thomas Knob Shelter. There were great views all around. A side trail to the summit beckoned while I paused to consider. The sinking sun made up my mind, and I turned away, saving that walk for another day. My path led off to some trees where a group was camping in the tenting area away from the shelter. I chatted with the guys briefly before making my way over to the shelter.

A herd of "wild" ponies had beat me to the shelter and appointed themselves as the welcoming committee. Obviously, they weren't really wild, as they clearly expected me to feed them. I had to shoo a way clear so I could get to the shelter. Immediately they came close to the shelter and stuck their heads in as far as they could reach. They were interested in licking everything—the rocks, the table, and the shelter itself. I was glad the shelter was well up off the ground or the ponies might have just followed me in. Damn big shelter mice!

The water source was a foul-looking little pond. I used both my filter and Aquamira, a chemical water treatment, just to be sure, and found myself wishing I had gotten some of that nice clear water that I had before the summit trail. That water had looked much more appetizing.

I made dinner and settled in for the night. All through the night I heard the little noises from the ponies, stamping, swishing, and chewing—that, and the wind sighing through the trees.

Firsts

Preston Lee Mitchell   **Northbound**
Wapiti Shelter, VA
April 24, 2009

This past week was a week of "firsts." I completed my first marathon day, hiking over 26 miles. It was pretty tiring, but the trail grade has been easier in Virginia so it was a more reasonable day than expected.

I also had my first solo shelter night on the trail. Usually I welcome the solitude and have tented alone a couple nights by choice, but I think because I was expecting to see other hikers at the shelter I was kind of lonely. I was also a little freaked out because the one night I happen to be alone at a shelter, it's at the infamous Wapiti shelter. Wapiti shelter is known as "murder shelter" because two seperate murders have occured there throughout the trail's history. Turns out both murders were by the same man, who is now locked up in jail . . . I think. Afterthought: Maybe this is why no one else showed up to sleep here for the night.

Another "first" was night hiking. I guess thru-hikers get tired of the same routine everyday so we think of new activities to spice up our life on the trail. "Hey—Let's try hiking at night!" It makes perfectly logical sense—hiking the Appalachian Trail in the dark when you can't see any scenery. I thought I would try it anyways. So after dinner was finished, I packed up my gear, strapped on my headlamp, and started hiking.

I decided I actually love night hiking. First of all, the temperature is much cooler, and at dusk, the forest really comes to life. I must have seen ten deer plus an owl and a turkey that nearly gave me a heart attack. I didn't realize the turkey was even there until it loudly flapped its wings and flew right in front of me on the trail. I actually screamed out loud.

As dusk turned to night, the setting became more eerie. I started walking through a really dark and creepy pine forest that was unatturally quiet. Eventually the remaining dusk light was gone so I turned on the headlamp and could no longer see anything except the stars above and whatever my headlamp was shining towards. Now I know you readers are not ready to jump out of your seat from suspense right now, but trust me, walking alone in remote woods during the night is really thrilling. Something about it really got my blood moving and it was kind of scary. I kept thinking about the *Blair Witch Project* movie, minus the witch (hopefully).

So after 26 miles of hiking, 8 of which were in the dark, I arrived to the infamous Wapiti murder shelter around 10 P.M., all alone. Yes, all these "firsts" happened on the same day.

After sleeping with one eye open all night, I awoke to a beautiful day and I'm now alive and well in Pearisburg, VA. I think next time I hike at night, I'll try and recruit a fellow hiker to do it with me.

Snakes and Hitchhiking, or Living Like You Were Dying

John Bitner (Churchill)   **Southbound**
Rockfish Gap, VA
October 21, 2010

I stepped on a snake. I was hiking along merrily, minding my own buisness, and then I stepped on a snake. The whole thing transpired in three seconds. Worst three seconds of my life. They say the average thru-hiker on the AT takes five million steps, so let's assume I've taken three million. Three million times my feet have hit the ground. I know what ground feels like, and my foot had not hit ground.

There was a guy in New York who told me that snakes are terrified of humans. Baloney. I would like someone to hook a snake to a cardiac monitor and see if it goes into atrial fibrillation when it sees me, the way I do when I see it. If I saw two snakes certainly I would go into a fatal heart rhythm and require cardioversion or worse.

So it all happened in a few seconds. It went something like this: Hmmmm . . . that doesn't feel like ground under my foot . . . (insert six expletives) . . . snake hiss with tongue thingy . . . it's a freakin' copperhead . . . my heart rate 400 million beats per minute . . . jump back a little and redirect snake with trekking pole as it tries to strike me . . . now I gain confidence . . . stomp on snake behind head and hold it there with my foot . . . drive the working end of my trekking pole through its little snake head . . . watch as helpless snake slithers its last slither . . . place my other foot on tail end of snake, reach down with trusty pocket knife and cut snake in half just to be sure . . . put snake head in ziplock baggy to show my friends what I had done.

George Washington I am not . . . that was all a lie. I saw a snake and almost stepped on it. I screamed louder than an eleven-year-old girl at a Justin Bieber concert. I got more air than Michael Jordan jumping back six feet. I looked at the snake and begged and pleaded—can we talk about this? The snake slithered into woods . . . and then . . . I cried.

I had another unforgettable experience—a much better one—yesterday while hitchhiking. Hitchhiking is an essential part of hiking the trail. Very rarely does the trail actually dump you off right inside a town with everything you need. It usually drops you off about 5 or 6 miles down the road. I hate hitchhiking; it's not even that familiar to me, since I'm from New Jersey where it is illegal and would almost certainly result in your death. My first hitch was in Rangeley, Maine. We all piled into the back of pickup truck whose driver was nice enough to pick us up. Tater sat up front with the driver, who was smoking weed. You can't be picky when you're begging for a ride. I hitched out of Rangeley by myself.

When you're hitching, you almost want to hold up a sign with your intentions: "REALLY SMELLY HIKER REQUESTING RIDE TO TOWN . . . BEWARE, I REALLY SMELL, AND THANK YOU FOR YOUR GRACIOUSNESS" or "JUST SHOWERED IN TOWN LAST NIGHT, NEED RIDE BACK TO TRAILHEAD, AND I'M NOT EVEN A BUM BECAUSE I HAVE A REALLY NICE CAR IN MY DRIVEWAY BACK HOME." I used to profile the cars coming. This turned out to be a mistake. I originally would be looking for only dudes in pickup trucks. That way I could get in the back without stinking up the cab. After a while you just start sticking your thumb out for everything . . . after you wait long enough. In fact, I've even started dancing at times while hitching.

So back to my first solo hitch . . . after an hour I was losing hope and wondering how the 8-mile walk back to the trail was going to feel. Just then, a silver Toyota FJ cruiser pulled up. When I got to the window I was stunned to find a very attractive woman in her mid 30s. She was dressed professionally, and as I told her where I was trying to go she started to laugh and said "I know," as she extended her hand and introduced herself. When I got into the car she laughed and said "You don't even smell; I was prepared for the worst." She drove me the 8 miles back to the trailhead despite the fact that it was well out of her way to a meeting. We made great conversation and had quite a few laughs. Turns out that she had a couple of friends that had thru-hiked. They always make her pick up thru-hikers, explaining how hard it is to get a hitch, and now she doesn't even hesitate.

Anyway, on to my hitchhiking story from yesterday. When I got to the road leading to Waynesboro an older lady pulled up across the way. She asked if I needed a ride (I hadn't even put my thumb up yet), and I imagined that God himself must have just dropped this car, complete with old lady, from the heavens. She started explaining that her son had thru-hiked in 1996, and had told her if she sees a hiker with a pack along this road it's okay to pick them up. Her son Jeff (trail name Okeepa) died three weeks ago of a brain tumor. He was forty and was a biology researcher at UVA I could tell that this was a special encounter, and having this smelly hiker in her car was in some way thereapuetic to her. She began to tell some of his stories, and recounted things he had told her about the trail and his friends. Ironically, she was only in the area to take care of some buisness regarding his death; she actually lives about an hour away. It was at that very spot on the road that she had picked him up from the trail and he had explained it was okay to pick up hikers with packs. I thanked her for the ride, told her that she and her family would be in my prayers, and thanked God for such an encounter.

I love the song by Tim McGraw called "Live Like You Were Dying." I can't imagine dying when I'm forty and not having this hike checked off my bucket list. I am intimately aware of the indifference of death, but sometimes you can forget that it is coming one day. I think sometimes things happen to remind us to use our time wisely. I am thankful that at the age of twenty-six, Jeff lived like he was dying—because he was. We all are.

Shelters

Jennifer Ensworth (Thin Mint)   **Northbound**
Wayesboro, VA
June 2, 2010

I like staying at shelters. They're really great places for socializing, and they almost always have a water source, not to mention a dry place out of the rain. Recently I've had some shelter issues though.

The first occasion happened after an 18-mile day. Several of us arrived at the shelter around 8:30 with about 45 minutes or so left before dark. The shelter was full and there were a bunch of people tenting. When I arrived everyone in the shelter was already in sleeping bags. A bunch of us were cooking and there were a few who got out their guitars and played a bit of music. After about 20 minutes one guy in the shelter got up and quickly packed his things, said "I've had enough," and left the site. At this point it's still not dark yet. So everyone goes to bed and come 4:30 in the morning we all get woken up by someone screaming "Yee haw!" Apparently it was one of the guys in the shelter retaliating as he left in the morning. These guys regularly get up before dark and go to bed before dark. This is not typical behavior; most hikers go to bed when it gets dark at "hiker midnight."

So anyway, a couple days later I'm talking to another hiker and he starts to warn me about this wild partying group that was in front of us who stayed up until all hours at that shelter on that night. I realize he's talking about us. I also found out later that another hiker who camped just past the shelter to avoid the crowd was woken up that morning by the same guys before 5 A.M. They said something to the effect of "Time to wake up!" really loudly as they passed him. Part of me wants very much to retaliate and get them back somehow. Instead, I just hope karma catches up. If they

59

intend to continue their habits, though, it's only going to get worse for them, with more and more folks night hiking as the weather gets hotter.

This was a week with a lot of stuff packed into it. I did two 22-mile days in a row, my first time doing 20+ days back to back. My goal was to do 100 miles in five days. By day three I was on track with a 20-mile average. This included two town visits (one resupply and another just to get a cold beverage). That third night out we had a massive electrical storm; it reminded me of some of the storms I've seen in Tampa. Unfortunately on the morning of day four I discovered a problem—my pack was broken. The night before I'd noticed some unusual back pain, but I thought it was just soreness from the big miles I'd just done. This wasn't the case; my frame was broken causing the weight of my pack to ride lower and put more strain on my shoulders. I made a quick decision. It was a Friday before a holiday weekend and if I waited til my next town stop it might take a week to get a new pack. So I decided to stop in at Montebello.

Montebello isn't a convenient stop. The trail crosses this old dirt road, and when you arrive there you have over a mile to walk downhill. Then you get to a gate where you can call the B & B owner for a ride or continue walking 1.5 miles. When I arrived at the trailhead I called my sister to check my service. Moments later this truck drove up. It's hard to describe exactly how shocking it was to see a car up there. This road seemed undrivable. Anyway he slowed down and I asked him for a ride. He drove me all the way to the B & B. I later found out that a hiker only gets a ride like that once or twice a year; I happened to be at the trailhead just as one of four people with gate keys drove by. Now if I'd had a choice I would rather have gotten a ride uphill, but I was grateful for the ride.

I went to the Dutch Haus B & B, where they serve a free lunch to thru-hikers. I made a quick call to Gregory to figure out what could be done about my pack. I was thinking I'd have to get a shuttle into Waynesboro to the outfitter and show them my pack and then have to wait up to a week before I received a new pack. I talked to the rep and he made things so easy. The plan was that they would overnight a new loaner pack to me and then I would send them mine for repair. So I decided to have the pack sent to Waynesboro and suck it up with my broken pack the remaining 42 miles. I ate my free lunch and was back on the trail by 2 P.M.

I had a massive climb uphill so when I got to the Priest shelter I stopped in for a break. The sky was looking darker at this point and there were others at the shelter waiting for the storm to arrive. I decided to hang out for a few to see what happened. It started to rain slightly, along with some thunder and lightning, and more hikers arrived. Then it started to pour and the lightning got closer. Then it started to hail and even more hikers arrived to get out of the storm. The storm lasted for about an hour and by the time it stopped there were at least sixteen hikers crammed into a shelter that sleeps six. I later found out that Greendog, who was half a day ahead of me, was hit indirectly by lightning in that storm. I was grateful to have missed the rain, but I decided to press my luck and move on; I had only gone 7 miles at this point. So I made it about 5 miles before the rain started again. Then it started to pour, not as bad as the first storm, but it would not let up. It was also starting to get dark. Instead of putting my tent up in the rain (which I have yet to do) I pushed on to the shelter close to 2 miles away. I arrived after dark and I felt horrible for arriving late—the two guys there were sleeping already—but in the rain, etiquette is a bit lax. I quickly got my stuff together and within twenty minutes I was in my sleeping bag (which is a quick setup).

Here is when I had my most recent shelter issue. A half hour after I arrived (about an hour and a half after dark) these three section hikers showed up. I wasn't upset at the late arrival, how could I be when I had arrived late myself? It was what they did when they arrived that made me so mad. For the next half hour they fiddled around in front of the shelter, setting up their hammocks and getting settled. This whole time they had their headlamps on darting around in the shelter, making it impossible to sleep. Finally, the third hiker decides to set up his stuff in the shelter. He sets his stuff right next to me, which is fine. But then he proceeds to read for the next forty-five minutes to an hour with his headlamp aimed right at me. It was close to midnight before I fell asleep.

I took it slow the next two days since my pack was not allowing me to do big miles. I finally arrived in Waynesboro on Sunday. I made it to the outfitter and discovered that my pack had not arrived, which meant I was stuck in town until at least Tuesday, when FedEx started deliveries again. This was a very bad feeling. Luckily I ran into Spirit Walker who had plans to slackpack the next day and agreed to bring me along so I would not lose the whole weekend. Monday I slacked south 20 miles and Tuesday morning I called Gregory to check on my pack. It never left their office. So they claimed they would again overnight it to arrive here today. So here I am waiting for the outfitter to call me to let me know my pack is in. It could be as late as 3 P.M. But there are worse places to be stuck in town. I am grateful there is a hostel here and a free campground. I could be stuck in a town like Daleville with only hotels where I would spend a fortune waiting on my pack. Unfortunately, some of my friends have moved on and I will have some catching up to do.

It occurred to me yesterday that, as frustrated and irritated as I was, I am still having a great time out here. Even a setback like this is an adventure!

Trail's End

Bruce Nichols (BirdMan)   Southbound (Flip-flop)
Harpers Ferry, WV

I climbed up out of Delaware Water Gap in bright sunshine. Once on the ridge, the trail would run southwest for 8 or 10 miles without much change in elevation before finally dipping down 1,000 feet or so into the next gap and then climbing out to do it all over again. This part of Pennsylvania has an infamous reputation for its sharp, unpredictable rocks. The mountains here are composed of layer upon layer of hard sedimentary stone that, over the millennia, have tilted to the vertical and slowly eroded away. The ridgelines are studded with long stretches of exposed strata that have cracked and crumbled into a rocky jumble. The rocks are very unstable and even boulders as large as a living room recliner can tip unpredictably when stepped on. Navigating these sections of trail took unceasing care and concentration and left little time for observing the surrounding forest. Even where the trail was relatively smooth, bread loaf–sized points of rock would protrude through the surface and require constant vigilance.

When I first passed through Harpers Ferry back in July, a friendly hiker at the ATC office had offered to drive me to a local restaurant for breakfast and then back to the train station so I could catch the noon train into Washington, DC. This hiker, Sue Ann Cherneskey, lived in Pennsylvania, not far from where the trail passed through Wind Gap. We exchanged email addresses and I added her to my trail update list. As I got closer to Pennsylvania, I received an email from her, offering me a place to stay for the night and help in resupplying if I needed it. I decided to take her up on the offer and called a few days before entering Pennsylvania to arrange a pickup.

I dropped into Wind Gap on the Saturday the twenty-eighth of September and gave Sue Ann a call. She picked me up at the post office and we drove to her apartment, where I had a chance to shower and do laundry. Sue Ann was an occasional volunteer at Hawk Mountain Sanctuary, one of the best locations in the Eastern U.S. to view the fall hawk migrations, and suggested that it would be an interesting place to spend a few afternoon hours. At the sanctuary we stopped briefly at the visitors center, then walked the half mile to North Lookout. A small clutch of volunteer census takers and visitors made up of avid birders and curious tourists sat on the rocky outcrop. Binoculars dangled from straps or were pressed to searching eyes. When a bird was sighted its location would be called out and half a dozen experts would call back and forth till there was a consensus and the species that was being observed was positively identified. Another volunteer with a tally sheet would add this migrant to the record. It was a good afternoon for birds. In about two hours we watched four bald eagles, numerous ospreys, sharp-shinned and broad-winged hawks, kestrels, and a few other species sail by on a brisk westerly breeze.

I spent the night on Sue Ann's sofa, bought her breakfast at a local diner in the morning to say thank you, and was back on the trail heading south once again. Before long, I again encountered "Red Truck" and "Green Truck," a father and son who were definitely "hiking their own hike." Using a pair of pickup trucks (one red—dad, Dale—and the other green—son, Matthew), they would park at opposite ends of their daily hike and walk from truck to truck. What made this system interesting was that though they walked north along the trail during the day, they were actually headed south and would drive the northern truck south to a point that would let them walk north again the following day. I'd missed the "Trucks" during the last few days after the heavy rains coming out of New Jersey, but our paths crossed once again in one of the most unusual places along the trail.

On a long ridge above Palmerton, the trail passes through a bizarre moonscape of barren rock studded with the stark skeletons of bleached dead tree trunks. For decades, the valley to the west had been the home of a zinc smelter that had belched clouds of toxic smoke, which prevailing winds had wafted over this stretch of the trail. The zinc, cadmium, and other heavy metals had rained down on the mountaintop, turning it into a veritable wasteland. It was designated a Superfund site in 1983. As you approach this section, warning signs caution against straying from the trail and advise that young children and pets had better be left at home. The smelter was closed quite a few years ago and the land has just begun to show sparse signs of recovery, but this three or four-mile section of the AT provides stark testimony to the disastrous effects of unchecked industrialization.

The Trucks warned me of the steep descent into Lehigh Gap at the end of the AT Superfund zone. And the rocky jumble that dropped down to the Lehigh River lived up to their description. I had to pick my way very carefully down through a maze of loose, sharp-edged rocks and boulders while trying to enjoy the spectacular view of the valley below.

I'd found a plastic guidebook protector that I'd assumed had been dropped by one of the Trucks, and when I passed the parking lot where the red truck was parked I lifted the windshield to tuck it where it would easily be found. When I let the blade slap back onto the window I was surprised by an incredibly loud car alarm. I leapt back then looked around sheepishly. In a van nearby some telephone workers were eating lunch and I walked over to explain that I was simply returning a dropped item of friends and not attempting to break into the truck. Fortunately, the alarm stopped its howling before I reached the van and I delivered my explanation in relative silence.

For the next few days the Pennsylvania rocks were the main feature and experience along the trail. The walking was a bit tiring, requiring caution and making it difficult to fully enjoy the fall color that was seeping into the surrounding forest. It took two and a half days to walk the 45 miles back to Hawk Mountain, a distance that I had covered by car in just over an hour. In a shelter at the base of the sanctuary, I found the copy of the Peace Pilgrim book that I had first seen in southern Virginia. My trail buddy Clint had picked it up and carried it to Pennsylvania. He'd left a note inside the front cover recommending the book and indicating the pages of the passages referencing the AT. In the register I found several entries that spoke highly of the book and felt a wave of gratitude for the opportunity to be walking the trail in Peace's footsteps on the 50th anniversary of her journey.

The miles were rolling by. On October 4th I passed the 2000-mile mark on another rain-soaked day. That night, in Rausch Gap Shelter, fog pressed down on the wet earth and visibility was almost zero. I was surprised to awaken a little after midnight to the sound of geese flying overhead. Fog still wrapped around the shelter and I wondered if the birds were flying blind or sailing through clear air somewhere above the clouds. When I rose again a few hours later and ventured a dozen yards away from the shelter to answer nature's call, I was delighted to see stars overhead for the first time in several days. Morning arrived with glorious sunshine and cooler temperatures as I set out on one of the longer-mileage days of my journey.

I was anxious to get to Duncannon and the Susquehanna River. This was the spot that Mildred Ryder and her companion Dick Lamb had finished their flip-flop hike in October of 1952. Mildred, later known as Peace Pilgrim, was the first woman to hike the entire trail in one season; she went on to spend the next 28 years walking the country as a penniless pilgrim, spreading a message of peace to all she encountered. Mildred had been a great inspiration to me as I hiked the trail 50 years after her hike, and I tried to pass on her message of peace to the people I met along the way.

I was running low on food—a mixed blessing, since it meant my pack was getting lighter—and needed to do a little resupply. A couple days earlier I had to ask the Trucks to pick up a couple of bagels for me on their drive south when I realized I did not have enough of these lunchtime staples to get me to Duncannon.

I was also looking forward to spending a night in the Doyle Hotel, a place that has become an AT icon. Built around the turn of the century by Anheuser-Busch and run for many years by the Doyle family, the hotel had fallen on hard times and deteriorated. A new owner is trying to gradually renovate and restore the grand old building to some semblance of its glory days. But life at the Doyle still revolves around the bar and a somewhat motley assortment of characters make up the "regulars" and long-term residents of the Doyle. But a big banner hangs out front welcoming AT hikers, most of whom probably qualify as being a bit "motley" in their own right, and the price is right at $15 a night for a room with sheets on the bed and a clean towel.

I could have walked the 30 miles from Rausch Gap to Duncannon in a single day but opted to stop a few miles short of town and spend one more night in a shelter. I could walk into town early in the morning, grab a big breakfast at the truck stop the trail passed before the final road mile to the Doyle, and still have a whole day to take care of my town chores. I ate the last of my Lipton dinners and was left with a handful of granola and a Snickers bar to get me into town in the morning.

I didn't sleep well that night, but had the pleasure in my sleeplessness of watching a parade of stars slowly rise into and cross a large gap in the trees to the southeast of the shelter. First came the Pleiades, followed by Taurus and the bright star Aldebaran. Next it was the belt of Orion slipping out of the leafy branches and beginning its slow arc upwards. And finally, near dawn, brilliant Sirius, the Dog Star and brightest of all the stellar sky objects. I'd also seen two meteorites flash across the open section of sky in the opposite direction of the processing constellations. I'd dozed between sessions of sky watching and, though a bit tired in the morning, was energized by the thought that Duncannon was only a couple of hours' walk away.

The Trucks were just getting ready to leave a parking lot on the north side of the Susquehanna River when I walked out of the woods. We chatted a bit and I invited them to have dinner with me to repay them for their assistance earlier in the week. We agreed to meet at 6 P.M. at the Doyle and I struck out across the bridge that spanned the river. After breakfast at the truck stop, I walked into Duncannon on a sunny, warm Sunday morning. Like many working-class towns in the Northeast, Duncannon has seen better days. Many of the stores on the main street of town were empty, their dark and dirty windows staring out at the road like so many blind eyes. But the town folk were friendly and I received a number of "Good mornings" from people I encountered on the street and a few waves from passing motorists.

Arriving at the Doyle around 10 A.M. I discovered that the check-in time there is noon. That's when the bar opens and it is at the bar that all business at the Doyle is conducted. On the wraparound porch on the second floor a few hiker-types were sitting at a table reading the Sunday paper and sipping on coffee or beers. Seeing my pack, they invited me up. Two were indeed active hikers though one of those had managed to get side-tracked at the Doyle for most of a week. The other three had been at the Doyle for a considerably longer time. Two of those had originally been hiking but for one reason or another had settled in for longer stays at this run-down establishment. I gathered from the conversation that there were a number of long-term residents at the Doyle and they seemed to have become a makeshift family of sorts.

At noon the bar opened and after about another hour of delays, I finally got to drop my things into a funky room on the third floor. There were some unpatched holes in the wall where work on wiring or plumbing had been done. A bare light bulb hung from the ceiling, with a brown extension cord running from a socket in the light fixture over to the wall and then to another lamp. I didn't see any other electrical outlets in the room. The bathroom across the hall had a plywood floor and several layers of ancient exposed paint in various stages of peeling from the walls, but the shower had good pressure and the toilet worked—what more could one possibly want?

I walked down the street to the laundry, was offered a lift to the grocery store as my clothes churned in the machine, and finished my town chores in short order. At six o'clock the Trucks, Dale and Matthew, arrived and we walked down the street to a local pizza place where I ordered the "small stromboli" and was confronted with a folded-in-half pizza full of mozzarella and ricotta cheese and an assortment of vegetables that left me a couple of notches beyond full by the time I had cleaned my plate. Ah, the dietary immunity of long-distance hiking!

When I returned to the Doyle, I repacked my gear and crawled into the double bed that took up most of the small room. The mattress was a real piece of work. I'm not sure how old it was, but it was of some kind of innerspring construction and it seemed that all the springs functioned independently of each other. There were lumps and bumps and prodding protuberances liberally and randomly spread about the surface. By carefully arranging myself on a diagonal in a slightly contorted shallow S curve I managed to avoid the most obnoxious springs, but remaining comfortable proved to be a nightlong challenge.

Before dawn I was across the street having breakfast at a cozy lunch counter in the company of a section hiker who had also spent the night at the Doyle. I hung around the hotel for another hour or so after breakfast, then checked for mail at the post office, sent some no-longer-needed items home, walked the paved mile of trail out of town, and returned to the woods.

After Duncannon the notorious "PA rocks" dramatically diminish in number and the walking becomes more enjoyable. The perpetual ridges and gaps of northern Pennsylvania give way to some wonderful stretches of farmland across broad rolling valleys. After many days in the wooded hills it was quite refreshing to be walking across open fields and pasture with occasional pockets of bright autumn forest.

On the day I passed the 100-miles-to-go mark at Boiling Springs, I walked the first hour by the light of my headlamp in the starry darkness before sunrise. I encountered a number of deer that appeared as pairs of distant glowing eyes often followed by a percussive snort and the crashing of deer bodies through the underbrush. In the blush of first light I surprised a reclusive gray fox crouched in the middle of the trail and intently staring at some hidden animal presence just off in the underbrush.

As the day grew brighter, I had quite a surprise myself. I was approaching a wooden bridge that crossed a small stream when I heard running footfalls approaching. I couldn't quite see the far end of the bridge but heard the first few thumps of rubber soles on boards. Then whoever was running must have seen me because there was an abrupt stop and a bolt in the opposite direction. By now I could see the far end of the bridge through sparse branches and was astounded to see what certainly appeared to be a naked jogger dashing madly away in the opposite direction. I say "appeared" because the combination of early light and perfectly aligned branches made a positive ID not quite possible. But there was this large flesh-colored male torso and legs with dark hair and running shoes with just enough leaf intervening in critical places to leave me with only the slightest bit of doubt about what I was seeing. The runner quickly vanished around a bend and, when I subsequently rounded it and came out into a more open area, was nowhere to be seen (probably thankfully). An intriguing twist to this incident was that it was the first morning in which I had encountered frost on the trail when crossing some open fields in the predawn and the air had a bit of a cold bite in it. Not my choice for a gallop in the buff.

As the last miles wound down, clouds once again began to scud across the sky. Occasional rain showers would soak into the surface of the trail. The Trucks and I were back on the same schedule again and we would pass on the trail daily, they in their rain gear and I under my umbrella, exchanging greetings and impressions of the ground just covered. The woods were wet and fragrant with the autumn smells of damp earth and fallen leaves. At Pine Grove Furnace State Park I stayed in a Hostelling International facility that had once been the stately mansion of the owner of the smelter. This old stone colonial building provided a comfortable and authentic connection to the historic landscape through which I walked. The next night I joined the Trucks at their campsite in a campground in Caledonia State Park. This time they treated me to dinner and I got to sleep in the back of the green truck, a late-model Ford pickup that belonged to Matthew.

On the following morning I crossed the border into my fourteenth and final state, Maryland, in steady rain. The trail streamed with water wherever there was slope enough to let it run and sat in pools in the flat spots. My umbrella found lots of use. It kept the worst of the rain off me but did not help to keep my feet dry and I squished along in damp shoes and soggy socks. With the end of the trail only a couple of days away, I pushed on to make miles and covered over twenty-seven on that rainy day, for a three-day total of seventy-five. The rain came down in torrents throughout the night but I was dry in a new shelter with a neat sleeping loft. The shelter's water source was quite a distance away but I avoided that wet trip. I simply placed my cookpot beneath one of the steady streams that cascaded off the roof and soon had more than enough water for my needs.

In the last 30 miles the trail flowed over the rolling hills of Maryland. The climbs were never long and the trail, though continually damp, presented no serious difficulties. I spent my last night in one of the oldest shelters on the trail. It had been constructed in the early 1940s when the trail was newly completed. Almost a decade and the Second World War would intervene before Earl Shaffer accomplished the first thru-hike in 1948. As I spread out my thin foam mat and sleeping bag on the old boards, I wondered if Dick and Mil (Peace Pilgrim) had found their way here as they walked north to Duncannon in 1952.

When I awoke on Saturday morning, October 12th, I was filled with the emotion of beginning my last day on this old brown path. It seemed, at once, like such a long, long time on the trail and also like the briefest interlude. Had it really been over 5 months since I started out in rain at

Springer? Had I really walked over 2,100 miles? Was it just a coincidence that three of the main moments of my hike—Springer, Katahdin, and my final day on the trail—were shrouded in mist and cloud?

I still had a bit more that 16 miles to walk and decided to get an early start so I could finish in the early afternoon. During the morning I crossed two Civil War battlefields and stopped to read the display markers that told the story of the battles and their fallen soldiers and generals. Photos taken after the fighting revealed a landscape scalded by war and much different from the serene forest and fields through which I walked one hundred and forty years later. The historic sites gave way to a long, undulating wooded ridge that would ultimately slope steeply down to the Potomac River and the end of my journey.

I was overtaken by a couple of runners out for a long training run in the woods. They stopped and walked with me for a while, offering warm congratulations when I told them of the impending finish of my AT hike. I met them again at a parking lot after descending that last hill and just before beginning the final few miles along a flat canal tote path that led upriver to the bridge that would carry me over the Potomac into Harpers Ferry. We exchanged more greetings and they sent me on my way with words of encouragement and praise.

By now the morning rains had stopped but the skies were still overcast and threatening. The tote path was wide and flat and, on a Saturday a little before noon, should have been full of walkers, joggers, and cyclists. But the inclement weather had reduced their numbers and much of the time I walked with no one in sight.

About halfway along the three miles of flat walking before the bridge I became aware that my toes were beginning to feel sore on top. I'd been wearing damp socks for the last few days and the combination of wet material and water-softened feet had caused the tops of my toes to begin to chafe. I was so close to finishing I was reluctant to stop, but I knew that one last dry pair of socks was packed in a dry bag at the bottom of my pack. So I stopped by the side of the path, sat down on a damp rock, and emptied my pack till I located the dry socks. My feet were wrinkled, trail worn, and red from rubbing on the tops of the toes, but the dry socks were like a little slice of metatarsus heaven. With happy feet I reshouldered my pack and walked the last mile or so to the Potomac Bridge.

So here I was, after 139 days on the trail, climbing a set of metal stairs that led up to the bridge deck and my last mile on the AT. The emotions were really starting to get a grip on me. I started out across the river and stopped a family of tourists and asked them to take a photo of me on the bridge with Harpers Ferry just on the other side. As I turned and started walking again, I could feel the tears trying to find a way out of my eyes and the surge of a sob hunkering around in my chest struggling to escape into the atmosphere. I'm not sure what I looked like to the regular Harpers Ferry visitors—a scruffy, bearded gent in damp clothes, with a green pack on his back and a misty look on his face. I got a tentative grip on myself and made it across the iron bridge. The only thing left was to negotiate the small bit of trail in town and then find my way up to the bluff that would lead me back to the place where I had left the trail three months earlier.

When I descended the bridge and walked around the corner into the historic section of the village, I was met by the sight of hundreds of people milling about in the narrow street. Some were in 1860s costume; others, in modern dress. A reenactment of the election of 1860 was in progress and the town was packed with tourists attracted to this annual event. Because of the desire of the park service to keep Harpers Ferry as much like it appeared in the 1860s as possible, the use of white blazes to mark the trail is kept to the barest minimum. (Maybe "less than the barest minimum" would be more accurate.)

I found the blazes that instructed me to turn left into this seething sea of reenactment humanity, and walked slowly and somewhat dazedly along trying to find the next marker. I could see the bluff rising up to my right where I knew the trail must be but could find no indication of the trail's approach to it. So I just kept walking, thinking that the next marker would be just a bit further along. The road I was following led through the legions of tourists, out past some big tents where other events and refreshments were to be found, out past where the buses ferrying people in from the remote parking lots stopped to unload, out past the last of the outlying buildings, and along the underside of the bluff I wanted to be on top of. I kept looking for some indication of a trail that would lead upslope to my AT finish, but to no avail.

During this time my tender, teary, trail ending emotion was slowly transforming itself into frustration colored with just the slightest tint of hopping mad anger at the utter imbecility of the National Park Service who had made things so hard for this trail-weary AT hiker on the verge of experiencing the glorious conclusion to a heroic journey. My mood had been busted, scattered on this asphalt road like the damp October leaves that lined its edges.

I turned around and walked back into town, wondering where I had gone wrong. Along the way I even stopped and asked some park personnel about the location of the trail and got only the vaguest and most useless responses. When I got back to the center of the reenactment commotion I discovered how I had missed my turn. A very low pole at the end of a stone wall bore the two white blazes that indicated a right turn up the hill. Still sitting where he had been when I'd passed fifteen minutes before was a very large man munching on a bag of chips and practically leaning on the pole, which was completely blocked from view by his copious body. And on the other side, the park service had placed an equally huge garbage can that also hid the pole from view. It was only luck that had led me to see it when I stopped practically on top of it to scan the surrounding buildings for some indication of the trail.

Back on track, I started up the hill but soon had that same sinking feeling when no additional blazes were to be found. Then up the street among the throngs of tourists I saw two figures making their way through the crowd with packs on. We honed in on each other like bits of cosmic jetsam being sucked into the same black hole from opposite directions. "Do you know where the trail is?" we said almost in unison. After a brief discussion, we split up in different directions to ferret out the disappearing AT. I headed down a narrow alley that appeared to lead in the direction of the bluff that I knew the trail followed around the upper part of town. And there, at the end of the alley, on another very inconspicuous pole, I finally found another blaze. I tramped off, spotted "The Bears" down the street, and hollered loudly to them to follow me. And at last, the crowds were behind and a real trail underfoot.

I'd been reading the entries of this couple in the shelter journals for quite some time but had not expected to meet them. They were southbounders who had spent an additional day in town and were just trying to find their way back to the trail to continue on south into Virginia. I was glad to have their company and they were equally glad to be able to share my last half-mile on the trail. We talked a bit about our respective journeys and finally came a sign pointing up to the town above. I felt that this must be the spot where I'd climbed up to the ATC office on my walk north and we took pictures, shook hands, and hugged, and then parted company, they south on the trail and I up the slope, having finished my walk.

As soon as I got to the top of the hill, I knew I'd stopped just a little short. I walked along the top of the bluff until I came to another descending path and there, where it intersected the trail, found the pole with two blue blazes and a little sign with an arrow and the letters ATC, which I now remembered from my July 5th exit from the trail. I gave the pole a hug and took a couple more arm's-length photos of the true end of my journey and then walked back up slope and on to the ATC office. There, a little after my pole hug, I filled out the forms to officially record my hike of the trail, added a new entry to the register, and had my photo taken again. Since not many hikers finish in Harpers they put it up on a corkboard in the office

rather than in the photo binder on the table. On the same board was a photo
of Pete Harley and GiGi taken on January 1, 2002. Pete's had been the very
first photo in the book that year. I talked with the office volunteers about
my encounters with Pete on the trail and learned a little more about the circumstances of his death in the Whites.

A group of about fifteen Girl Scouts arrived and I became the focus of
an impromptu question-and-answer session about hiking the AT. I don't
know who enjoyed it more, the girls or me. Afterward we went out front
and took group photos, exchanging cameras and swapping places so everyone could be in at least one shot.

George, a volunteer in his 80s, offered to drive me over to the hostel in
Sandy Hook when the office closed at 4:30. All the beds were taken by a
large group of Boy Scouts who were on a Civil War tour over the Columbus Day weekend, so I slept on the floor in the common room. When I
walked back into town on the following day, I did walk that little bit of trail
I had bypassed on the hilltop. It turned out to be exactly 525 steps from the
first sign to the blue blazed pole. But as far as I was concerned, my journey
was complete when I wrapped my arms around that inconspicuous post on
Saturday. It wasn't the soaring alpine summit of Katahdin, but for me it
was equally as grand. A dream become real after a walk of 2,160-some
miles. A journey through both time and space, and also a journey of spirit.

Georgia on My Mind

John Pugh (Johnny Swank)   **Southbound**
Harper's Ferry, WV—Mile 1,165
10/26/2000

F inally back in the South, or close to it.

Hey folks! Sorry to have a lapse in writing but the computer access problem crept up again in Pennsylvania. Let's see, where to start? Well. I'm sitting in Harper's Ferry, West Virginia, having walked through Pennsylvania and Maryland to get here. About 1,165 miles down, with 1,000 or so to go. I passed the halfway point on 10/22. But that's getting ahead of myself, so I'll back up...

I left Delaware Water Gap after a wonderful visit from Anne and her grandmother with sort of a heavy heart, I'll admit. Sometimes hiking out here mirrors life at home pretty closely, with both good days and bad. Sometimes the weather's crappy, food is marginal, sleep gets thrown off, or something else comes up and you just have to deal with it or get off.

Anyway, the infamous Pennsylvania rocks didn't turn out all to be that big of a deal. It seems that for every tedious mile, there was an easy mile of old forest service road to walk on. And Pennsylvania was wonderfully flat in many areas. So nice. Anyway, I leave Delaware Water Gap and run into some of the folks from Backpacker Magazine doing a photo shoot, on *food,* no less. To top it off, these fine folks gave me a bowl of the leftovers to eat. Thank you Jonathon Dorn and Company for the pick-me-up!

Continuing on down the line, the AT comes across the Palmerton EPA Superfund Site. There was a zinc smelting plant in operation in this area for 80+ years. In the process, it seems that all plant life for about 10 miles of so

73

was completely wiped out. It was something like walking through a war zone. Incredible. They're in the process of trying to bring the area back to life by dumping Ecoloam on the hillsides by helicopter. This was the second EPA Superfund Site on the trail. The other was Nuclear Lake in New York.

The trail went back to normal after that, passing through several small towns along the way—Port Clinton, Duncannon, and Boiling Springs among them. Boiling Springs is named after a natural, spring-fed lake in the middle of town gushing out 25,000+ gallons a day to the river system. It was Friday night, so while I was in town I went to the local high school football game. I had to, because the any school that goes by the name "The Bubblers" has to get at least a look-see. Actually they have a great team, 8-0, with one of their kids getting a full ride to play football a Maryland next year (Derek Miller). To prove this visit had to be fate, one of the marching band's first songs was "Georgia on My Mind." Coincidence? I think not.

Getting to the halfway mark meant one thing—getting my initiation into the Half Gallon Club at Pine Grove Furnace State Park. This is a hiker tradition that goes way back. Here's the deal. You get to the park store, buy a half gallon of ice cream and if you can eat it in one sitting you get a wooden spoon embossed with "MEMBER OF HALF GALLON CLUB" stamped on it. I think I froze my brain and came close to seeing my lunch a few times, but hey, I GOT MY SPOON, MAN!

Statistics: Half Gallon of Hershey's Chocolate Ice Cream
16 servings
140 calories per serving (2240 calories)
80% calories from fat
240 grams sugar
434% daily allowance of saturated fat

I didn't eat dinner that night.

This entire area is steeped in history. Part of the trail goes by several major battle sites. I drank from the same spring Benjamin Franklin drank from when he supervised the building of a lookout post for Fort North-hill. When I drank from the spring, I seemed to feel all of Ben's inventive-ness and intellect coursing through my veins. Then I realized I was just dehydrated.

Camp David comes fairly close to the trail in this area. I tried to find it to get a full briefing on the current situation in the Middle East, but it appears that I was not on the guest list. I'll have to have my people look into that matter.

All of the monuments in this area give me pause to think of all the battles fought in these hills. Amazing to walk to same ridges thousands of soldiers fought on.

I'm starting to put together a list of trail terms I hear a lot out here and will be writing that out in the next few weeks. The first term, though, is one of my own. P.M.R.—Permanent Music Replay: the occurrence of getting the same song stuck in your head for days on end. This is not to be confused with P.B.R.—Pabst Blue Ribbon, a fine domestic beverage that is both tasty and light on the wallet.

P.M.R selections of the last few weeks (in no particular order)

"Roxanne Roxanne," UTFO
"Make It," Aerosmith (It's the first tune on the first album.)
"Folsom Prison Blues," Johnny Cash
"Baby Got Back," Sir Mix-A-Lot (a poet, and artist, and a fine man)
"Say You, Say Me," Lionel Ritchie (This haunted me for days!)
"R.E.S.P.E.C.T.," as sung by Aretha Franklin
"Aqua Boogie," Parliament Funkadelic
"Smells Like Teen Spirit," Nirvana
"Hootchie Cootchie Man," Muddy Waters
"Stranglehold," Ted Nugent
"Couldn't Stand the Weather," Stevie Ray Vaughn
"Cracked Actor," David Bowie (The cutoff *Live at the Tower Theater.* Wow. Just . . . wow)
"Third Stone from the Sun," Jimi Hendrix (I'll never get tired of this tune.)
"Night Life," Willie Nelson
"You Were Born to be my Baby," Bon Jovi (I don't know why, please make this one stop!)
"Thunderbird," ZZ Top (My oldest sister Mitzi gave me this tape [*Fandango*] for my thirteenth birthday. Although the tape long gave up the ghost, it's burned into my memory quite deeply.)

Whew! That's a bunch of rambling stuff to throw into one update. Thanks for bearing with me. Tonight I'll cross the border into Virginia, where I'll be for about 475 miles or so. Almost feels like home.

Oh, You Should Really See a Doctor About That . . .

Karelyn Kressler (Little Dipper)   **Southbound**
Harpers Ferry, WV
September 4, 2009

While hiking through Pennsylvania I had begun to notice a large, hard, and painful spot developing on my tookus. I couldn't actually see most of it due to its location, but I could see the edge of it, and it was red. Oh man, was it red. A tick bite, I thought?

On several occasions I would catch myself pouting with my eyebrows furrowed, and with one hand rubbing my malady (which I will remind you was on my rear end). I was checking to see if it was still there, if it still hurt, if it had shrunk, etc. . . . Maybe it would go away as quickly as it came, like a cold or a bruise. I was sure one day I'd feel for it and it would be gone, and I'd think, "Huh, I wonder how long that's been gone." It occurs to me now that others may have also caught me in this affectionate rub to my behind. I wonder what they thought. Did they think I was lonely? I wonder if the concentrated look on my face threw them. But no matter.

When I stopped in Duncannon, and then went home to Bloomsburg, bringing six trail friends with me, I had the chance to look at myself in a full-length mirror. It was still there. It was red, and looked like a bull's-eye, but not the kind I had seen in photographs of tick bites. There were concentric rings of dry skin. It was sore, hard, and raised. It had grown larger since I first noticed it, and there were two sizable bite marks in the center of the inflammation.

A spider bite? *Eh, I've been bitten before, and I don't feel sick. It'll probably pass.*

These were the thoughts I used to comfort myself. I didn't have health insurance and I was worried that if I showed someone my tush, in particular my mother, I'd be forced to get off the trail. However, you don't *become* sick in the doctor's office. You're already sick and the doctor is the one who has to clue you in. I needed to get a second opinion.

While we were at my house, my trail mate Fiddler asked to go to the emergency room. The doctor reported that Fiddler had a small hernia and a skin infection. Antibiotics would fix the infection, but the hernia would eventually require surgery. Those things don't just fix themselves. Fiddler looked at me, worried. "Aren't hernias for someone . . . older?" he asked me. I didn't know. Fiddler was nineteen, and fresh out of high school. He looked like he wanted his mom. I wanted his mom too.

If he didn't seek surgery, the doctor told him that bending over and picking up heavy things could make it worse. So basically whenever he bends down to pick up his pack he's going to have to worry about literally ripping a new one. I was worried that he was going to have to go home, seek surgery, rest up, and possibly not make it back to the trail with enough time to finish this year.

This is what comes of telling doctors you have problems. They give you a condition.

But I showed my mom, the retired nurse, anyway. First, I encouraged her not to get excited. Then I dropped my shorts. She said that we should call the tell-a-nurse right away.

Great.

The tell-a-nurse told me to start using a topical antibiotic, such as Neosporin, and to seek additional help if the swelling didn't go down. I crossed my fingers, and hopped back on the trail.

A week later it was still there. It was hard to sit down and I'd nearly start crying whenever my arse took any sort of a hit.

Yeti, a southbounder I had met in Maine that had since left the trail, came to pick a few of us up in Harpers Ferry and took us back to his house. Papa Yeti and his good friend Susan gave us the best breakfasts. I watched Planet Earth for the first time, and enjoyed their showers. At such a nice place, the group had decided to "zero" (take a day off, a day where you hike zero miles) and I thought, "Okay, it's now or never." So after breakfast, I decided I would seek not only a second opinion, but a second, third, and fourth opinion.

Not too long after the dishes were washed, I walked into the dining room and asked the guys (Curse, Yeti, Lost Rob, and Bacon) if I could show them something on my badonkadonk. They all said yes without reservation. Hey, it was a free show! I decided not to drop my shorts, but instead I just lifted up the side. And upon this exposure the guys started groaning and I could almost hear them reeling back and flinching with disgust. Someone said, "Dipps, you should really see a doctor about that!"

Now, this is the last thing you want a guy to say when you reveal something so sensitive, such as your butt. You'd rather hear, "Nice!" or "Damn, that one fine booty." But no, they told me to show it to a medical professional . . . that I needed help.

So, through an amazing connection of Yeti's, I got into see a doctor for free (I beat the system). I was led past all of the waiting patients and seen within five minutes of my arrival. What service! The doctor told me it wasn't a tick bite. I had been bitten by something else and had developed a minor staph infection. I remember he said the word "MRSA," which freaked me out, but he assured me that I didn't have that and not to worry. He wrote me a prescription for an antibiotic that was on special (free) at the local pharmacy and wished me luck. Though I thought my luck was looking pretty good right about now. Thank you, doctor.

And thanks to Travis (Curse) I finished off my medication, and the bite disappeared. My bum is once again looking quite fine.

P.S. Bacon, I don't think you're ready for this jelly.

Swallowed by the Forest

Deb Lauman (Ramkitten)   **Northbound**
Tumbling Run Shelter, PA
June 29, 2000—Day 90
Total miles: 17.4
Trip miles: 1050.6

Lunch break at Pen-Mar park. I'm sitting in a pavilion, looking out over my current home state of Pennsylvania. As soon as I leave here, I'll cross the Mason-Dixon line.

As I walked along this morning, I was engrossed in my imagination and didn't notice the clearing just ahead of me. Suddenly, I heard a train that sounded like it was right there in the woods. I looked around as I continued to walk and, moments later, emerged from the trees and found myself looking at pavilions, benches, and dozens of picnic tables. A train was passing by below, at the bottom of the grassy hill.

In 1878, the Western Maryland Railroad opened this park, which, in its heyday, was known as the Coney Island of the Blue Ridge. A Lutheran picnic around the turn of the century drew 15,000 people. The *Thru-Hiker's Companion* also says that facilities in the park once included a three-story hotel and an amusement park. The park, as it used to be, ceased operation in 1943. Says here that remnants of the former resort are visible along the AT, south of the park. Hmm, I must have been really deep in thought; I didn't see anything.

I've hiked a little over nine miles so far today, with 8.3 to go. Let me tell ya, there's nothing quite like the feeling of putting on soaking wet clothes, socks, and boots first thing in the morning, but the only way to get them dry, unless you hang them on a line in the sun for most of a day, is by wearing them. My shorts, t-shirt, and sports bra are now dry, with the exception of a little sweat, but my socks never had a chance in those wet boots. I just couldn't bring myself to put on cold, wet undies this morning, so those are still soaked, too. (Oh, that didn't sound so good, did it? They're soaked from yesterday's *rain,* you see.)

So, anyway, we asked the park caretaker if we could hang some things out to dry on the gazebo railing while we ate lunch, and he said that was okay. Just after we did, however, we heard a rumble of thunder, and the rain started falling once again. Figgers.

Not long after I started out this morning, the trail crossed a power line. We've crossed many over the last 1,000 miles. I'm always unnerved by the electric buzz and crackling, and I walk quickly across the clearings. But this morning the power lines only hummed, and I paused before going back into the woods on the opposite side. The rocky trail continued into the trees, but it just didn't look right. I noticed some trodden grass to my left, which followed alongside the woods and the power line and an underground gas line. I didn't see a white blaze in any direction. Logic would generally dictate that the trail would continue straight ahead, back into the forest, as it usually does. Something told me to turn left, however, and walk parallel to the power and gas lines. I did so for a few minutes, still not seeing any blazes, and the trampled grass continued with no other trail turning into the woods. Then I saw it a hundred yards or so ahead—a white blaze nearly hidden by underbrush. Instead of going into the woods, the trail actually continued along the power and gas lines for a distance of maybe a third of a mile before turning into the trees again. I'm starting to think you develop A.T. radar or some kind of sixth sense about the trail.

I also wanted to mention something I saw at the A.T.C. Headquarters. Remember a ways back I saw a tree eating a sign, and all you could see of the sign was the word "Trail" with a horizontal crack through it? Well, hanging on the wall of the A.T.C. was a framed photo of the same tree. The difference was that it was obviously taken quite some time ago, because the word "Appalachian" was still visible and the "mouth" of the tree had just begun to close over the top and bottom of the sign. I should have asked when that photo was taken, so I'd know how long it has taken the tree to consume nearly the whole sign.

I think it's amazing how the forest swallows things. Today, the trail took us over an old stone wall, which indicated that the area was probably once part of a homestead. I recalled the remnants of Sarver Cabin in Virginia and what was left of another abandoned house that trees had started to engulf as the building fell to ruin. Some things take a long time for the forest to eat, while others aren't digestible at all. (Many of those indigestibles are left in the woods by hikers and campers.) On the other hand, development swallows the forest at a much faster rate. It takes decades for a tree to eat a sign or a century for a forest to obscure a house, but virtually no time at all to build a road or subdivision where trees once stood. You're very aware of that fact when hiking the A.T.; it's anything but remote in many areas.

Well, lunch is about over and, yay!, the sun is out once again. There are still big, white, poofy clouds around, which could very well mean more rain and thunder-boomers, but, for now, there's blue sky, too. That means it's time for me to walk.

7:30 P.M.:

We have left the AppaLATCHun trail for the AppalASHUN Trail, as we've crossed the Mason-Dixon Line out of the South, into the North. I've lived in Pennsylvania for only two years now, but I guess it's grown on me; I feel like I walked into home today. Funny thing is, the trail seemed to change with the states. I don't quite know how to describe that one, but it looks different somehow.

Funny little story to tell you . . .

Split P went to the restroom at Pen-Mar park, where two young girls, maybe ten years old, occupied two of the stalls. Split P goes into the third. One of the girls leaves her stall and approaches the sink, where she sees Split P's partially-filled water bag. Keep in mind she uses iodine to purify, which turns the water yellow.

All of a sudden, Split P hears the little girl exclaim, "Eeew! Eeew! Brittany, c'mere! You gotta come look at this!"

Brittany answers from her stall, as the first little girl starts making gagging noises. "What is it? Are you throwing up?"

"No! Just c'mere!"

So Brittany flushes and goes to the sink. In a half-whisper, the first girl says, "Ew, its one of those pee bags!"

"Eeew!" they both whisper loudly.

Split P, listening from her stall, interjects, "That's not what that is. That's not pee, it's iodine." She then exited her stall and explained.

A bit later, as Split P and I were heading out of the park with our packs on, those two little girls and their camp group of maybe eight more ten year olds were sitting nearby. Split P walked over to show them that she really was drinking the yellow liquid. I followed and stood off to the side. Split P was instantly surrounded by little girls asking lots of questions. Interesting thing: They didn't ask the usual questions most adults ask. Instead, they started off with, "How do you go potty in the woods?" followed by "What do you wipe with?" and "What are those blue things around your ankles?" She was referring to our gaiters.

Before long, I too was surrounded by little girls.

"Do you get a reward or medal when you finish?" one of them asked me. When I told her we don't, she wrinkled her nose and said, "Well, you should. But I guess you'll feel good about it, though."

"Yes," I replied, *"That's* the reward."

I couldn't help but notice that the girls standing around me kept glancing from my face to my chest. I was wearing only my sports bra—you know, like when you go to the gym. I imagine they were either thinking, *How do I get me a pair of those?* or *Geez, I hope I don't get those!*

Well, dinner is ready and this is one long entry, so that's enough for today.

The Half-Gallon Challenge

A sign stood before me that read: "Springer Mtn–1090.5, Mt. Katahdin–1090.5." I had finally made it to the halfway point after three months and a few days of plodding along. How did I feel? Ecstatic. Excited. Overwhelmed. How did I celebrate? The only way I should. I ate a half gallon of ice cream.

It's thru-hiker tradition to stop in at the Pine Grove Furnace State Park, located a couple miles past the official halfway point (this year it was 1090.5, but the trail changes in length each year and only seems to be getting longer), purchase a half gallon of the flavor of your choice of Hershey's ice cream, and down it, in its entirety, in one sitting. A half gallon is four pints, which means I would have to eat the equivalent of four Ben and Jerry's.

I had to participate, of course, but I had some things going against me. I got sick a couple weeks ago and since then have been on anitbiotics that have completely eliminated my hiker hunger. My spork had snapped in half in my peanut butter the night before, which I figured could only be a bad sign. And I don't even like ice cream. But if you know me, you know how competitive I am. I was going to will myself through this one.

I got to the park in the morning after hiking about 7 miles. I had purposely skipped breakfast to leave as much room as possible. I was excited to see that Snake Farm and GPS were already there and letting their ice cream blocks thaw out in the sun. I quickly purchased my half gallon of Neapolitan (didn't want to get tired of one flavor) and set it out with theirs. I had so much adrenaline pumping, I was ready to kill a lion—or just demolish a whole bunch of ice cream. GPS was focused and Snake Farm was a little more relaxed, smoking a cigarette and cracking jokes.

18 minutes and 30 seconds in. GPS gobbled up his last bit of Peanut Butter Swirl. The crazy Lithuanian dominated his half gallon like it was finger food and exclaimed he could eat more. He went inside and got a ham, egg, and cheese sandwich and a coke. I looked down and I was maybe one fourth of the way done. My brain was already telling me to stop.

39 minutes in. Snake Farm and I were struggling. We had moved out of the sun into the shade, and were having to take long five-to-ten-minute minute breaks between every couple of bites. My never-ending brick wasn't getting any smaller.

50 minutes in. Snake Farm was visibly about to get sick. "You better not throw up!" GPS yelled through a mouthful of some other food he was making fun of us with. I was doing jumping jacks and running around, trying to get my belly to digest some of the frothy, creamy mass. I needed a different taste in my mouth. I went over to the soda machine and got a Sprite.

51 minutes in. The Sprite allowed me to take two more bites. My ice cream was melting at an alarming rate and a chocolatey strawberry soup was forming at the bottom of the box. I still had a pretty good-sized lump of strawberry ice cream left, with the chunks of strawberry giving me the most trouble.

An hour in. I was ready to be done. I finished up the last of the solid ice cream, gagging with each bite. I just had a small cupfull of melted ice cream left. It was sure to ruin milkshakes for the rest of my life. Ice cream had already been ruined. Strawberries were definitely coming close to be ruined, too.

67 minutes. I drank my last sip of ice cream soup and slammed my cup down. Snake Farm had his head down on the table and GPS and some others had already lost interest or given up on us. "Ahhhhh!!" was all I could let out, as the others realized I was done. I had succesfully willed myself through one of the most miserable food experiences of my life.

Two hours later, I finally strapped my pack back on and hiked out of Pine Grove. I'm pretty sure I'm lactose intolerant, although I think anyone is intolerant to that much. But I did it!

On to hike the second half to Maine! I will surely finish—just as long as I don't have to eat a full gallon at the end.

Episodes

Corwin Neuse (Major Chafage)   **Northbound**
Bear Mountain State Park, NY

One may encounter numerous hazards on the Appalachian Trail, including severe weather, ravenous man-eating black bears, ravenous man-eating hillbillies, mosquitoes, ticks, deer flies, chiggers, spiders, steep grades, limited water, contaminated water, contaminated raspberries, poison ivy, giardia, disease, southbounders, and lethally venomous snakes.

Conspicuously absent from that list, however, is "dodging traffic while running frantically across a four-lane divided highway during rush hour." Yet that is exactly what I found myself doing on this particular morning, much to my considerable dismay and consternation. It was kind of exciting, though.

What's that? You expected me to say more? Oh, well . . .

Early that morning I found myself in the unenviable position of having the cross the Palisades Interstate Parkway, a four-lane divided highway. During rush hour. And, unlike at virtually every other "dangerous" road crossing on the trail, the powers that be had inexplicably neglected to provide a bridge. Or tunnel. Or crosswalk. It seemed one simply had to wait for a break in the traffic, and then run for it. Easier said than done, especially when your knees are shot and you're carrying a preposterously bulky forty-pound backpack.

I can only imagine the mirthful confusion of motorists as they watched me dance nervously by the shoulder, before I sprinted (or, more accurately, waddled awkwardly) out into the road in front of them. In a moment of astonishing clarity, I was struck by the fantastic serendipity of my successful pre-breakfast privy run when—as I suddenly became hyperaware of the inexorable inertia of the several thousand pounds of angry metal screaming towards me—my bowels involuntarily loosened. Even so, I somehow made it safely across the road, body intact and compression shorts unsoiled.

Only to realize I had only made it to the island between the southbound and northbound lanes, and that I had to repeat this entire terrifying process all over again. And so what should have taken me fifteen seconds ended up taking more like fifteen minutes. Or indefinitely, as I may have actually died somewhere along the way, and am dictating this narration to my (clearly unflappable) next-of-kin from purgatory.

I caught up with Hobbit on my way up Bear Mountain. I hadn't seen him since Maryland, when we ran into each other while he was attempting the Four State Challenge. We chatted for a bit, catching up, commiserating cheerfully over our myriad individual failures.

Bear Mountain was underwhelming, and then infuriating. Underwhelming because the park was chock-full of clueless tourists who had driven right there to the summit, inadvertently undermining my (admittedly already meager) sense of accomplishment. Infuriating because the soda machines by the central observation tower were prohibitively expensive, and most of the marauding day-trippers didn't seem to understand my pitiful attempts at yogi-ing. Even when I sat in plain view, staring pointedly at the sun with parched lips aquiver. Well, except for a kindly middle-aged couple, who gave me a spare bottle of water.

Water.

Ugh.

Descending Bear Mountain was a treat, and then absolute torture once I reached Hessian Lake. A treat because the trail down had just recently been reopened, and now featured a series of newly constructed, languidly twisting, wide stone stairways. Torture because approximately ten thousand people were having loud parties and barbecues and picnicking around the lake. Munching on enormous bags of crisp, crunchy potato chips. Tossing back ice-cold beers from their coolers. An intoxicating haze of smoke rising from innumerable grills. The audible fizz of freshly popped sodas lingered in the air, drowning out the blissful laughing of the children.

And yet nobody seemed to notice me, the shockingly emaciated homeless man walking through their midst. Despite the deafening rumble of my stomach. And my comically round eyes, as I stared in transparent envy at the buffet around me.

I might as well have stripped naked and danced around singing La Marseillaise, for all the attention I was getting. Well, except for that I can't speak French. Irritated beyond belief, I kept my head down and exited the park as quickly as possible.

The Bear Mountain Zoo was a quaint, mercifully brief distraction. I can't say I appreciated seeing all these wild animals I'd already seen on the trail locked up in cages, though. That was mildly depressing. But at least the zoo had water fountains.

A sign hung alongside the walkway greeting me as I approached the bridge over the Hudson River.

"WARNING!" it angrily proclaimed, "Nesting Peregrine Falcons are extremely territorial, and may dive bomb your skull at any second. Say your prayers."

The Peregrine Falcon is often referred to as the world's fastest animal, capable of diving at over 200 miles per hour. Getting hit in the head by a particularly well-thrown fastball can be near fatal, and a baseball weighs only five ounces; I shuddered to think what a two or three pound bird could do to me flying at twice that speed. It wasn't exactly like running across a busy highway, but crossing the bridge was similarly thrilling. If I had to go out—if a falcon had to kill me—at least I would die awesome. (Or should that be awesomely?)

Once across the bridge, I looked back for any signs of the birds. I had no idea what I was looking for, but could see no evidence of any nests on the suspension bridge's tall towers. And the sky above me was clear. Well, except for. . .

It flew in from the north, looking initially like a peculiar, rather ungainly seagull. But then it was much too large to be a gull, and only its head was clearly white, the rest of its feathers a weathered russet brown. It definitely wasn't a falcon, but it soared like one, gliding majestically past me and over the bridge.

I felt a chill run down my spine—and a twinge of admiration, or something vaguely like pride—that I didn't understand at first. It was a Bald Eagle.

A couple miles further on, I was back in the woods, and had just discovered a cooler of sodas and beer left by a German day hiker. What a thoughtful man. I couldn't decide what would satiate my thirst better, a Heineken or a Coca Cola. I settled on both. It was . . . interesting.

At the end of the day, after an easy but eventful fifteen miles, I found myself at a convenience store on US9, waiting for a ride. One of my girlfriend's coworkers, Chelsea, lived in nearby Cold Spring, New York, and had offered to put me up for the night. I drank a couple of Mountain Dews while I waited, anxious but excited to get into town, eat real food, talk to real people, and sleep in a real bed.

Chelsea was very nice, and she and her husband extremely forgiving and accommodating. I assume I must have smelled like a week-old corpse, and not looked much better, but they graciously invited me into their home, allowed me to do my laundry, gave me juice, and let me use their computer. Unfortunately, they had a prior social engagement, or else they might have enjoyed picking my brain for stories and wisdom about the trail. And I would have enjoyed telling them.

Ultimately, I ended up walking alone to the grocery store in the dark. My resupply here was much more sensible—and lighter on the fluffy, fake chocolatey things—than my previous one had been in Jersey. On a whim, I purchased a quart of chocolate milk from a local farm. And drank the entire thing before I had left the parking lot. Delicious.

I went back to Chelsea's house, checked my e-mail, and tried to stay awake as long as possible, in case they came home and wanted to talk. But hiker midnight (eight or nine o'clock, for you normal folks) came and went, and I found myself slipping into an uneasy unconsciousness. I knew I would have another long day ahead of me—and then only two more until home!—so I quickly packed up and turned in, falling almost immediately to sleep.

CT and Now MA

No Promises (Julia Tyler)
Dalton, MA
Saturday, July 24, 2010

Northbound (Flip-flop)

Connecticut was thick with tall pine trees. The scent of pine was so strong I hoped it would stick to my clothes and work as deodorant. The red pine needles on the forest floor gave me a bounce in my steps. In these woods, morning sun rays streak through the pine trees, and as the wind blows, the trees' shadows on the ground look like a kaleidoscope turning.

My incredible family came and hiked with me for a week through these forests. I savored every second with them, on and off the trail. But now that they're gone, I only miss them more. I miss Mom's ecstasy over a clean pair of socks. ("New socks?! I feel like a new person!!") I miss Will imitating Mom imitating a thru-hiker (head down, hunched over, bobbing up and down, big steps). I even miss Will and Ellen laughing about farts late into the night. Every night. (Their trail names are appropriately "Lard Butt" and "Butt Face," respectively. They politely used each others' names at every opportunity.) I miss Dad and his punny humor and and his steady, congenial presence. My dear family! Come back! Luckily, wonderfully, my brother Calvin is joining me for some time before he heads back to Germany this fall.

Anna C. came out too! And "Shake Down"! "Shake Down" may insist she's not thru-hiker material, but she's joining me again in a few days, so we'll see . . . Their company was like water on a hot day. I had missed the company of people who already know and love me. People who have to love me! People who know good food and make a scene about good food like I do. People who take smirking pictures like I do. (Anna, did you *see*

89

that photo of us?) People who give me hugs and back massages. They say you need ten hugs a day, so I had been short on hugs for nearly two months!

One of my favorite moments with the family was on the second day. We were short on water and the few stagnant streams we did pass were not drinkable even if filtered. We decided to push on a few more miles to the next clean water source. Only minutes later, we encountered trail magic. A thru-hiker from 2007 left us clean water, cookies, and watermelon with a note saying "Trail Magic."

Trail magic may sound campy or hokey, like the trail names, but before you judge, I challenge you to come out here and sweat and stink. Then you can decide how you feel about trail magic. Plus, once you hear a few burly, bearded men praising trail magic, it may sound cooler to you, as it is.

After our dose of trail magic, Mom, "Mama Bear," had the generous idea to give back to the trail. I'd grown used to being the needy recipient, so it hadn't crossed my mind that I could be, instead, a trail angel. A few days later, we brought plums, Oreos, and water to a road crossing on the trail. We felt positively great about ourselves. I'd like to do that more often. Maybe I could live somewhere near the AT, like the Cookie Lady I passed yesterday. The Cookie Lady makes about 1,500 cookies during the summer months when hikers pass by and stop in to her house. I met the Cookie Man and told him he was a lucky guy. He agreed.

Since my family left, I've entered into Massachusetts. The first person I encountered in Massachusetts was a man on a motorcycle who drove past me on a road which crossed the trail. He was cranking "Cecilia, you're breaking my heart!" I got the feeling Massachusetts was going to be a good state.

Other than these darned mosquitoes, I've been right.

Earlier this week, I decided to take a day off from hiking, and work at Moon in the Pond Farm in exchange for quality organic food, a shower, and a place to pitch my tent. The farm reminded me of the movie *Babe* or E. B. White's *Charlotte's Web*. Animals were everywhere. Geese, ducks, chickens, and turkeys wandered around like they owned the place. The roosters tried attacking me and the farm intern, Matt, a bright-eyed high school sage. I also met Bri and Josh, two earthy and earnest farm apprentices, who are committed to their garden beyond reason. Josh dreams of the weeds growing in his sleep, and Bri will fight any fight to help her vegetables grow. I admired all three of them.

I could've gotten sucked into staying longer on their farm with their company, but I am committed to my hike. I've got to travel on. And with each day northbound, the mountains get steeper, the trees get taller, and the views get more breathtaking.

On one mountain top view, the song "America the Beautiful" rose up in me. It's easy to become cynical, what with all the heartbreaking injuries to Earth, like oil spills and mountaintop removal, but this hike is making me fall back in love with the United States. We have spectacular beauty here. I am overcome with gratitude for the people who have protected areas of the U.S. like the Appalachian Trail.

O beautiful for spacious skies,
For amber waves of grain,
For purple mountain majesties
Above the fruited plain.

On the AT, I've walked through amber waves. I've walked over purple and blue mountains. I've stared up at the spacious skies. At night, that sky has made me aware we are hurtling along at a crazy speed, in a lonely universe, and I've clung to the ground as though I'm on a roller coaster.

And actually, this journey has been very much like a roller coaster. The ups and downs come faster and harder than I could have imagined. And I'm hanging on as best I can.

Laugh Louder

John Bryant Baker (Sunshine)   **Northbound**
East Branch of the Deerfield River, VT
7/7, Day 107

My feet hurt. My knee hurts. They are not sore. They don't just ache and they aren't just stiff. They hurt. My feet are calloused and blistered. My heels are both bruised and tender to the touch. Where the nail of my right pinkie-toe used to be there is now . . . well, I don't really know what that is. My knee is swollen. I touch it with my index finger and can feel the fluid that has built up around my knee cap. 107 days, 12 states, and over 1600 miles of walking have taken their toll. I gently rub and massage them after another long day on the trail, mainly out of obligation, feeling guilty for what I've been putting them through. Sometimes I imagine them looking up at me and yelling obscenities, asking what in the world I am thinking.

"Why were we not a part of the decision-making process?" they ask. "You wanna walk from Georgia to Maine, fine, sounds great . . . just as long as you walk on your hands."

My imagination begins to wander. Then I remember a story, a story of a woman. She was also attempting to thru-hike the Appalachian Trail, and, as every thru-hiker is at some point or another, she was asked the question, "Why? Why are you out here?" Her reason was somewhat shocking. Shortly before starting her hike, she was diagnosed with terminal cancer. Her doctor had given her months, a year at most, to live. She said she wanted to be on the trail because every day that she was in the wilderness, every time she struggled to make it up a mountain, every moment of pain, every step, was another moment that she knew she was alive.

I've found that I understand her answer a little more each day. It's when I'm pushing up the last few feet of a steep climb, sweat completely saturating my shirt and still pouring down my face, and just as I reach the summit, I am greeted by a gentle breeze that manages to send a chill down the length of my spine. It's bending down over the coldest, clearest spring I've ever seen, cupping my hands, and tasting its refreshing purity. It's standing atop an exposed ridge, trying to comprehend the magnificence of the sunset that is on display before me, and all I can do is throw my arms out wide and scream. It's waking up to the beautiful songs of birds and falling asleep to the soothing hoot of an owl. It's when it rains so hard that all there is to do is laugh. It's waking up on the morning of our 5th anniversary and looking at my wife asleep next to me. We're in our tent, on the Appalachian Trail, living out a dream that was just some crazy idea we began talking about when we were engaged. These are the moments that remind me I'm alive, the moments that remind me that I am blessed.

A friend of mine once shared with me his analogy for life. He explained to me this idea of how life is like a big sponge that is totally saturated, and that the harder we squeeze, the more life pours out onto us. I've thought about the picture for a while now. I've often envisioned myself squeezing every last drop of life out of that sponge. I want to squeeze so hard, so hard that it hurts . . .

I look back down at my feet, realizing I have a new understanding of my friend's analogy. Maybe they're not yelling obscenities at me after all. Maybe they're just trying to remind me that I'm alive. Maybe it's not about being comfortable, but instead thriving in the uncomfortable? Maybe it's about embracing the struggle instead of trying to find an easier way? As I lie back and slowly begin to drift to sleep, I think about the experiences, the moments, and the adventure that still lies ahead. Such a gift life is! I hope I can always remember this truth. I hope I will always remember to live life 'til it hurts and to laugh louder the harder it rains.

The Good and Bad of Extracurricular Hiking

John Bitner (Churchill)   **Southbound**
Gorham, NH
August 1, 2010

Happy birthday to me!! I'm in Gorham, New Hampshire, having now completed Maine and 297 miles of trail. Maine didn't let us go easily; in fact, it chewed us up and spit us out.

We are staying at a place called White Birches trailer park, which is full of old guys who park their RVs here in summer and in Florida in winter. I am sitting around a fire with a bunch of them now. When older folks find I'm an ICU nurse they feel compelled to yell me their latest lab values from the doctor, their prostate function, and their surgical history. In exchange, I guess their social history and medications they are probably on. I lecture them on the importance of actually taking their meds and why their blood glucose level is so much more than something more their Doctor can nag them about. I believe in holistic nursing; nursing is part of who I am and not just a job. You don't have to be wearing scrubs to make a difference. I enjoy this, and I enjoy them.

I've made some new buddies. Stoker (Jarred) and Wolfman (Louis), both from North Jersey. They were frat brothers who just graduated Penn State. Their birth on the trail goes something like this. Wolfman was researching hiking when he came across the AT online. In a drunken conversation he tells his buddies he is going to hike it. In a drunken melée of

94

zealousness Stoker says "Sure, I'll hike it too . . . hahaha." The next morning, a hungover Stoker knocks on a hungover Wolfman's door and says
"Hey, I got nothing to do this summer, let's talk about this hike." They are
great company and are my style. Ample breaks and naps are part of the
routine, as is swimming at every oppurtunity.

On one particular afternoon, we stumbled upon a blue-blazed trail that
led to a waterfall. I should explain something: Along the trail there are
other trails with blue blazes that often lead to special interests . . . vistas,
cliffs, summits, waterfalls, etc. Now this would be considered extracurricular hiking. There is nothing we enjoy less than hiking "extra." My feeling
is that the AT is 2,179 miles long. There is plenty to see in 2,179 miles
without doing extra. On this day, however, we opted for extracurricular
hiking at the prospect of swimming. What we found was the kind of place
I envisioned when I dreamed of hiking the trail. Two waterfalls, a deep
swimming hole, and big rocks to jump off. We had a blast.

After a couple hours stoker mentioned that if he could find bait he
could catch a bunch of fish there. Yeah, right!! You're a Jersey boy, Stoker,
what do you know about catching fish in a hole in Maine? I told him if he
caught a fish then I would eat fish for the first time. He pulled out a pill
bottle with fishing lines and hooks and fashioned his trekking pole into a
fishing rod. He started splitting logs until he found grub for bait. Don't you
know, that kid caught eight fish!! Brook trout. He gutted it, and that night,
I ate fish. That kid is freaking MacGyver. He has mad woodsman skills . . .
and from Jersey? In fact, he has taken up whittling. He fashioned a wooden
figure that we have named Wilson (see *Cast Away*). Wilson has a conniving
grin and a Pinocchio nose. He is godlike and we have declared him the
knower of all things. He hates us mostly. We ask him for advice and input,
and we imagine he reminds us we are fat and lazy and need to hike.

One day I accidentily took a blue-blazed trail down a mountain. I was
a mile and 1,000 feet down before my daydreaming stupidity looked up
and saw the wrong-colored blaze. I could have cried. This was not only
extracurricular, but an extracurricular descent and climb. That's the worst
kind!!

We celebrated Christmas in July. I declared July 25 Christmas and
declared my trail name "Father Christmas" for that day. We sang carols and
exchanged stories of family traditions. I also declared I could announce
Christmas at any time I wanted. Sometimes you just need a little Christmas.

"Tater-isms." This is a term we fabricated to keep track of funny lan-
guage, stories, or words Tater chip uses. This will become a staple in my
trail journal. Tater chip carries bear spray. This is funny to us because it is
generally considered useless on the trail. Tater explains, "Well, heck, the

spray ain't for the bear. If I see a bear coming at me I'm gonna spray myself cuz I don't wanna see what he's fixing to do."

When hungry, Tater might say, "I'm so hungry I could eat the north side of a duck flying south." (Translation: I could eat a duck's ass.)

These guys are my trail family—can you see why I'm having such a great time?

Vermontages

No Promises (Julia Tyler)　　　　**Northbound (Flip-flop)**
Hanover, NH
Wednesday, August 11, 2010

Rutland, Vermont. Calvin "Big Bunny" and I find each other in the one-room airport. We make a scene laughing and hugging. We regress back to our teenage selves. He starts making fun of me. I pretend to beat him up. People start staring at us. We leave.

First night out: Young math teacher at shelter wonders at our loud happiness as we make dinner. He asks if we are dehydrated. We ask if he ever gets crazy. He fumbles with words for awhile, then says, yes, absolutely.

That night, "Big Bunny" and I stealth camp in a very unstealthy location, right next to the trail.

Second evening out: We get ice cream at Gifford Woods State Park. A ranger teases us that we are crazy, and asks if we are dehydrated. We rebuttle, and yes, she also gets crazy sometimes. Then, we stealth camp again, in an equally unstealthy site a few miles from the campground.

Third day out: "Big Bunny" and I reach the top of a mountain as the sky opens up and lightning shoots down. I flop onto the ground, as if to avoid the bolt. "Big Bunny" laughs at me, drops pack, rips off sweaty shirt, beats chest, and hollers out to the sky. We are literally on top of the world. We can see miles in all directions, and we can see the hefty grey clouds racing towards us. My lips are tingly. Lightning strikes closer; I scream and break into a run down the other side of the mountain. My brother laughs more. I ask him, I beg him, to please come down this 4@*j!z mountain right now, because we're going to die. Resistantly, he follows me down into the pine forests.

Rain like you can't imagine starts pouring down. It's not individual droplets of rain. It's like a lake is emptying onto our heads. I start laughing hysterically. The weather is comically bad. "Big Bunny" gets sullen. He reminds himself he'll be on the beaches of Southern France in three days. I apologize on behalf of the rain. Many miles later, we drag ourselves into the next shelter. We have to cram seven of us into the six-person shelter.

"Big Bunny" sleeps next to "Croft" (Lara). "Croft" snores raucously and sleep talks when she isn't snoring. We listen to many sensible conversations that night, ranging from cell phone reception and bills to logistical planning and issues that are "not [her] responsibility." "Big Bunny" eventually hunts around in the dark for Benedryl to knock himself out.

The next morning is understandably difficult, but as the day warms up and dries out, our spirits brighten. We walk through foggy woods, through mist rising from the night's rain. We see thousands of spider webs glistening from the moisture in the air. We see bright red lizards, and big fat toads, and an unbelievable variety of mushrooms. "Big Bunny" says this forest is magical. He takes off his shoes and hikes the last six miles barefoot.

We cross the river into Hanover. I cheer, waving my trekking poles like a lunatic, thrilled to be in New Hampshire. The big, bad White Mountains are on my horizon, and Maine waits just beyond.

I am ending in Maine this year, instead of returning to Harpers Ferry and finishing the southern half of my flip-flop hike, for several reasons. Primarily, I am tired. This is hard. I have exhausted all my reserves, physically and emotionally. I still have 441.8 miles left to Mt. Katahdin. That is a lot. I have mixed feelings about it all, but I do intend to complete, to feel, and to be further transformed by these next 441.8 miles.

I wanted to do something difficult for the sake of difficulty (thank you, Rilke), and I am doing it. Life willing, I will have walked with a thirty-pound pack up and down mountains for nearly 1,200 miles. And some day, I may hike the other 1,000 miles. But no promises.

My well wishes to all of you, and to the challenges and paths you all are walking.

The Sky Is Falling, the Sky Is Falling!

Amanda Redpath (Veggie)   **Northbound**
Hanover, NH
July 22, 2010

After several pints of delicious Long Trail Ale and a scrumptious veggie burger at the Inn at Long Trail where I wrote the last entry, I headed across the street where the Inn let thru-hikers camp for free. I encountered three awesome hippies living out of a tent and their truck—Mo, Otter, and Molly—and spent the evening chatting with them and doing some stargazing when the clouds passed. We chatted well past hiker midnight and they helped me finish the rest of the cookies that mom sent me in my drop box.

The next morning (Monday), I went to grab a cup of tea and charge my iPod at the Inn and I met two Sobo brothers. I had a nice relaxing 10-mile day to the Stony Brook Shelter, so for once, I took my time in the morning and didn't manage to leave until nineish. The sky looked like it was about to open up and vomit from the humidity hitting its gag reflex. It did rain on me a bit, but the trees took most of the brunt. I passed the Maine Junction where the Long Trailers go towards Canada and the ATers go towards Maine. Finally, I don't have to have any of the ridiculous gear conversations while I'm trying to eat. They were the same conversations from the first week in Georgia. I DON'T CARE ABOUT YOUR BLISTERS. I just want to eat my damn dinner. After I passed the junction, I circled around Kent Pond and then down to Thundering Falls only to a steep 1300-foot climb to no view and a bumpy ridgeline which then dropped into Stony Brook

Shelter, where I spent the night with three older women from Florida—Miller Time, Archy, and Tuna. About sixish the humidity finally fully hit the sky's gag reflex and the sky vomited very violently for about half an hour.

The next morning, I was woken up by the early-bird old people shuffling around as soon as the sun barely got up. Funny because Miller Time and I managed to stay in bed about forty-five minutes longer than the old people and still get out and hiking before most of them. I did a nice 15-mile day to a random stream about a quarter mile up off of a road and found the awesomest little place for just my tent. That was right after a rather large bumpy section and some Vermont Maple Soda (which actually only had three ingredients, none of which was high fructose corn poisoning, in it). It was very peaceful camping by myself because then I could sit and read my book undisturbed for two hours and then sleep for a solid almost eleven hours. I was amazed when I woke up the next morning and it was just before 8 A.M. When Popeye passed me after I ate breakfast, he had already done 6 miles. Whatever. I left about 9:30.

This started my train of Sobo sightings, amounting to seven Sobos from Katahdin in just one day. It was like snake sightings, but with people. I met LoneStar, who told me about a secret in Hanover which I might go explore, then Mother Goose, who was the first woman to yoyo the AT. What an interesting morning! I felt like I climbed for the first 6 miles straight. Then I hit the Thistle Hill Shelter where I went to go eat lunch. Right as I was finishing, it got really dark and thunder rolled across the sky like someone getting sucker punched in the stomach and you hear them hitting the ground—*thud thud thud.* So I took a long lunch break and waited out the storm. I didn't even have to go find the stream a quarter mile away because some nice person went and had some in gallon jugs and there was half a gallon left. I poured a liter in my Nalgene and went to use my Steripen water purifier and had my final straw with the piece of shit. Then I busted out the Aquamira. Give Steripen three or five years and they might get it to work right. I'm not convinced; it works when it wants to. Major Chafage waited out most of the storm with me there as well, then we trudged 5 miles to West Hartford where we walked through part of the town on the trail, which conveniently went right by a "Village Store."

Now this was not any village store. It was like we had time traveled—or rather teleported (albeit with no floo powder)—to Georgia. First we get there and sit with Zen and Devo and eat some bananas, chips, powerade, etc., and then we get a show. It can be in a little scene as follows:

Kid, obviously underage, tries to buy a case of beer.

Clerk: IDENTification please.

Kid: Crap, it's in the car.

Kid goes back to car while the clerk puts the beer back in place shaking her head. ENTER older scruffy shirtless man.

Old Scruffy Shirtless Man: Can I buuuy this here case of beer?

Clerk: NO. If you wanna bring a kid to buy beer with you, I ain't gonna sell it to ya. It's illllllllegal to have him ridin' with you and me ta sell ya this beer.

Old Scruffy Shirtless Man: Awww c'mon man . . . it's just a case a beer.

Clerk: Geeet outta here, I ain't sellin'!

LEAVE old scruffy shirtless man. ENTER two other shirtless men five minutes later.

Shirtless #2: *(Picks up a case of Bud Light.)* Whhhat arrre ya doin' givin' him shit for?

Clerk: *(Freaks out.)* Ya'll gonna run me outta business, that's what!

Shirtless #3: *(Picks up a case of Twisted Tea.)* Ya gotta sell ta somebody!

Meanwhile Carrie Underwood, Taylor Swift, and other apparently popular country songs play in the background interrupted by a "severe weather warning" for exactly where we are sitting.

Anyway, then Major Chafage and I hiked 4 more miles up to the Happy Hill Shelter. He got slightly ahead up me on one of the climbs up there and then it got dark. Like *dark* dark. Severe weather? Closing in . . . *dun dun dun.* The wind went nuts and I had to dodge several branches that seemed to be aiming for my head. I hike faster. It's still uphill. Thunder thunder thunder. The sky gets sucker punched in the stomach. Small open field. Shit, I have metal. A sign. "Podunk road," then "Shelter 1 mile." Get me out of the open! Up and over Happy Hill. I hear rain coming from a distance, just like the storm I waited out that afternoon. I start running. It was a good third of a mile that I ran and only got sprinkled on. I get to the shelter (the almost full shelter) and *bam!* Lightning and downpour. Helllllll yeah. Made it!

Then I heard from two Sobos that the shelter's water was dried up. Well, I had a little less than a liter. That wasn't going to be enough to get me through breakfast, so I collected another liter and a half off the roof and treated it. Good thing it was raining.

Last night was a full shelter which had some weekenders talking about the most ridiculous shit, from LeBron James to fashion week in NYC. They disturbed my thunderstorm listening. I just wanted to hear the rain. But no. They did eventually shut up. And surprisingly, they were still snoring when we got up.

Now I'm in Hanover, NEW HAMPSHIRE. Wooooooooooooooo.

A Thru-Hiker's
Motivation:
Not Enlightenment,
Just Ice Cream

Francis and Lisa Tapon   **Southbound**
Hanover, NH (Dartmouth College)
July 23, 2001, 4 P.M.

We made it! We're in Hanover! Besides Springer Mountain (the AT's southern terminus), Hanover is probably the most significant milestone for a southbounder.

Why?

It's a common saying that when a northbounder gets to Hanover, he or she has done "80% of the miles, but only 50% of the work."

For a southbounder, this is good news, because while we may have only done 400 miles, they represent almost 50% of the effort required to complete the AT. Maine and New Hampshire are the toughest two states on the AT. If you can get through them, you can get through the whole AT. There are no more major physical hurdles, only mental ones.

Indeed, the key challenge from this point on is psychological.

Can our minds stay engaged and positive as the trail meanders up and down the mountains between here and Georgia?

Will we let the relentless heat and humidity get to us?

How long can we last until we get to the next pint of Ben & Jerry's ice cream?

Speaking of which, we stopped at the Ben & Jerry's here in Hanover and asked if we could have "the white blazed special" (AT hikers follow white blazes all day long). The woman behind the counter smiled and gave us each a White Russian ice cream shake (with a bunch of goodies thrown in)—FOR FREE. Indeed, Ben & Jerry's gives this to all thru-hikers. We love them. In Glencliff, Lisa ate a whole pint of Concession Obsession (caramel, vanilla, peanuts, etc). What astounded her was that she wasn't even full. She felt good. Really good. So good that she ate a little bit of my Cherry Garcia pint.

We plan to see the movie "A.I." tonight, but first, we need to get our second helping of Ben & Jerry's.

Francis has been eating so much food, it's absurd. In fact, when we took that one day off in the Whites to help heal Lisa's blisters, we ate at an all-you-can-eat restaurant for breakfast, lunch, and dinner. But since we weren't doing any exercise, this proved a bit too much for Francis's digestive system. So for the first time in his life, he threw up because he ate too much food.

After a short break, he was packing it in again and eating everything in sight. He spreads butter on everything, desperately trying to consume as many calories as possible.

What's crazy is that he has still managed to lose *two* pounds. He now weighs only 143 pounds. Since he was 16, the least he's ever weighed was 145.

In fact, CBS is running a program called "Unsolved Mysteries: Where does all the food that Francis eats go?"

The Whites of New Hampshire were spectacular. We once again found ourselves above the treeline, exposed, while a lightning storm rocked nearby. Although we were rained on, we fared well and the lightning didn't fire over our heads this time. My GoLite umbrella helped keep me dry from the waist up, but my legs were wet (which is okay since they're always moving and generating heat).

The winds of Mt. Washington are infamous. Indeed, the highest recorded winds in the world have been on this very peak (231 MPH!).

The winds broke apart the storm, so that by the time we hit the tallest peak in New England, the skies had cleared completely and we sat on top of the world at 8 P.M. with a glorious sunset, 50 MPH winds, and visibility for hundreds of miles.

We hiked down, and just got to a warm hut called Lake in Clouds. There we agreed to help prepare breakfast for the guests and clean up in exchange for shelter and leftovers. Considering the weather outside (windy and cold), it was a good deal!

We will enter Vermont tomorrow. Therefore, we have finished two of the fourteen states on the AT. But as we said, they are the two hardest, and we expect that we will "fly" through the next dozen.

Our packs are now lighter than ever (seven pounds without food and water). We have traded our 20-degree bag for the lighter 40-degree bag. We sent back the parka and rain gear (in exchange for lighter umbrellas). We also sent back gloves and a few other clothes. In short, we sport some of the lightest packs on the trail. Fellow hikers are amazed and extremely curious about how we pull it off.

Our next major stop is Manhattan! Yes, NYC! Lisa has never been there, and we plan to tour around for three days (and have Ben & Jerry's everyday).

But that's a few hundred miles from here, so until then, you can all join us in breathing a sigh of relief for getting to Hanover.

It feels good.

Beginning Anew

Beef (Elizabeth Zane)   **Southbound**
Hanover, NH
September 1, 2008

Everything has changed.

Flamebo, Default, and I left Franconia Notch on August 13th for five days off trail. When we got off the trail we were soaking wet and exhausted in body and spirit. In case you haven't been following our blog, it had been raining every blessed consecutive day for forty days. A few days earlier Siren—one of our original group planning the thru-hike—had left the trail for personal reasons, which further dampened our mood. And to make matters worse, I was dealing with a serious bout of giardia, which I am pretty sure I picked up in Argentina while doing some AT conditioning. This nasty little intestinal parasite was starting to wreak havoc on my stomach. I was stuffing the side pockets of my backpack with Tums so that I could pop them into my mouth without losing a step. One sad day after returning to the trail from Andover, Maine, I threw up $10 worth of town food on the side of the trail. I had to ask Flamebo and Default "What is the leave-no-trace policy for vomit?" We decided leaf burial would work.

I ate a very light dinner that night to keep down the stomach discomfort. However, it turned out to be tough balancing nausea and weakness from lack of calories. The next day was particularly dreary. That afternoon, I found myself alone on a steep, wet descent down Twin peaks in the White Mountains. Flamebo and Default were behind me, since they had stopped to eat lunch; I had decided to skip it since the very thought of food still made me feel ill. The descent was slick but I felt unusually light. (Perhaps

105

I was a bit light-headed more than light-footed!) With the hut almost in sight, I took a spectacular face-first fall, landing with my pack pushing my face into a rock on which I chipped two teeth, split open my lip, and mangled my glasses.

I got to the hut and immediately went to the bathroom to examine my wounds. I couldn't help but notice that I looked like a prize fighter. I treated myself to tea and attempted to straighten the frames of my glasses with a pair of pliers.

I never considered my commitment to the trail, but I did question my sanity for holding onto it even as it proved itself often painfully difficult and anything but fun. While the high-intensity bonding born of shared suffering is real, it seemed at times that I was paying a high price for my AT memories. There were bright moments during these days which stand out like stars in a dark sky—the kindness of my family who rescued us for a few days during our trek through the rainy Whites, our one patch of clear skies between Lake of the Clouds and Mitzpah, and the warmth and hot food provided by the huts—but despite these reprieves, most of our days were spent being wet, cold, and disheartened.

Stepping off the trail on August 13th, we were whisked away into the arms of our community in Middlebury, Vermont. All three of us had attended Middlebury College together and created lasting bonds with the place and the people surrounding the school. It was a time to enjoy the simple things of life. The sun shone every day. We rested without the pressure to run around town and accomplish tasks. We scrubbed at the mildew eating away our packs and replaced rotting shoes. We remembered the joys of civilization, from hot showers to the incredible friendships that have supported us for the last six years.

We were picked up, driven around, fed, clothed, and listened to. Some highlights were a family-style dinner at the home of Laurie Jordan, Middlebury chaplain and friend, and visiting our home church of four years, Memorial Baptist. Perhaps happiest of all for me, I got prescription medication for the giardia that worked remarkably fast.

Maria (as yet un-trail-named) arrived, fresh from New Orleans and ready to join us for the rest of our AT hike. She challenged my somewhat indifferent attitude about returning to the trail with her unbridled enthusiasm. She didn't seem fazed by our tales of rain, mud, gastrointestinal revolutions, and tough terrain. Her excitement was contagious and started to eat away at the frustration I had been feeling.

We experienced what you could call a fresh start, a second wind, or the turning over of a new leaf, on August 17th. As we headed south out of Franconia Notch the climb was gradual, the mud had almost completely dried up, and the sun was shining. We reached Lonesome Lake as the sun was setting and the hut crew gave us an entire pan of freshly cooked stuffed shells, fresh bread, and peach cobbler for dinner. The change of fortune was so abrupt it was hard to believe. I felt like I was tiptoeing around in my dry socks and shoes, hardly daring to hope that it was actually not going to rain. Could this be the same trail we had left just a few days earlier?

I cannot say that the following week was without challenges. We did walk in a cold rain much of the third day before climbing Mt. Moosilauke and slept with all four of us huddled together in one tent to keep warm. The wind at the summit must have been about thirty miles an hour and had me ducking to keep from being blown over in the cold mist. But despite these flashbacks to the darker days, we began to sense that the rain's grasp was finally loosening, the cold ceased to penetrate, and the aches seemed to recede as we hit a streak of sunny days and our path lead to gentler trails. As we walked out of the Whites it was hard to suppress the sense of accomplishment and absolute euphoria.

The Vermont Mafia began to sing. We had sung before to keep warm, to ward off fear, and buoy flagging spirits. But as we sauntered down the south side of Moosilauke, we were singing with light hearts for the sheer joy of being together and moving with purpose towards our common goal. We sang during most of our twenty-two-mile approach into Hanover, New Hampshire (our longest day yet!).

Ain't No Competition

Deb Lauman (Ramkitten)   **Northbound**
Kinsman Notch, NH
August 21, 2000—Day 143
Today's miles: 9.5
Trip miles: 1778.1

Today, Gaited Mule learned a valuable lesson: When you're above tree line in 40-mph winds, don't spit! I was hiking behind Web Breaker and in front of Mule when I heard Mule make a yuck sound. He yelled over the wind, "I spit some chew, and the dern mess, it done come right back at me!" He says he's going to give up tobacco upon reaching Katahdin.

It was cold on top of Mt. Moosilauke today, and we stumbled around some in the wind. The summit was in the clouds when we got up there at eleven A.M. Just before passing tree line, we ran into the first flip-floppers we've seen: Yahtzee and Kokapelli, whom I'd met in the Shenandoahs while they were still northbounders. (Flip-flopping means hiking one direction to a point, then jumping up to the other end of the trail and hiking back to where you left off. It gives people more time to complete the trail, as Katahdin usually closes mid-October due to the often harsh and dangerous weather on the mountain.)

Yahtzee and Kokapelli told us how cold and windy it was on the summit of Moosilauke, so we put on our jackets before continuing. North-bounder Bulldog still hasn't received his winter gear, so he practically ran past us in his thin T-shirt. "There's heat in the feet," they say. He was long gone when we got to the summit, as he headed here to Kinsman Notch to hitch back to Hanover, I'm told. Apparently, the box with his cold-weather gear finally made it there, so he's got to go back for it. He's been going ultra-light for a while, but, I'm tellin' ya, it isn't smart to be backpacking in the mountains at *any* time of year without at least some warm clothing. The guy has been cold now for a couple of weeks, I'd say, and refuses the jackets people have offered him in camp. No offense, but that's plain foolish pride, if you ask me. Not to mention irresponsible. There's a balance between lightweight backpacking and being safe. You shouldn't compromise your own safety.

Anyway, we met a yo-yo hiker, Albatross, today when we stopped at Beaver Brook shelter for lunch. He started at Springer on January 1st, thruhiked north to Katahdin, and then turned around. The sixty-something-year-old man from the Oregon coast (I'm guessing at his age) said he loves it out here as much today as he did in the beginning.

Today, I tackled the section I've had the most anxiety about. It may not make a lot of sense to those of you who are familiar with the northbound descent of Mt. Moosilauke, but I've had it in the back of my mind now for four months and twenty days. And this afternoon it was the main thing on my mind. Know what, though? It was long, slow, and tedious, but wasn't nearly as scary as it had been built up to be, both by people's descriptions and by my own imagination. There were a few hairy spots, but I took my time with a patient Gaited Mule behind me and made it down just fine. Mule said, "No hurry, Ramkitten. You just take care o' your business. This ain't no competition. The object is to get down in one piece, with nuthin' broke or messed up." Amen to that.

Unfortunately, though, it was Mule who fell a few times. As he put it, there was "nuthin' broke and no blood," but he bruised some ribs on that last spill. If it had been raining, though . . . man, that descent would have been really tough! As Mule stumbled along, he provided today's Mule-ism: "I'm as coordinated as a bow-legged elephant with ingrown toenails," he said. I was sure happy to walk out into the parking area with Moosilauke and an intact Mule behind me.

What a huge difference elevation makes! It was comfortably cool and sunny back down at the bottom. I turned around and looked up at the puffy clouds drifting over a summit I could no longer see. Hard to believe what it was like up there. Like night and day.

The three of us walked a quarter mile up NH 112 to Lost River Gorge, where the snack bar people give thru-hikers an unofficial 40% discount, so we'd heard. What we'd heard turned out to be true, and we ate well for very little. What a pleasant surprise! After dinner, we found ourselves a legal throw-down site back towards the trail. On this chilly evening, we're at the edge of a meadow surrounded by mountains. I'm keeping my fingers crossed that our luck continues and the precipitation holds off. We're told it was minus 3 degrees on Mt. Washington today, and it snowed up there yesterday. Brrrr.

Flamebo Searches for the Rainbow

Devon Parish (Flamebo)   **Southbound**
Franconia Notch, NH
August 17, 2008

I used to love rain. Freshman year of college, I remember making a "Rain Songs" playlist on my big Dell desktop that included (among other fab tunes) "Let it Rain" by Michael W. Smith, "When the Rain Comes" by Third Day, and "Bring on the Rain" by Jo Dee Messina (these say a lot about who I was freshman year). While living in Vermont, I often went outside when it rained. I loved the idea of rain being God's way of sympathizing with tears, and the more drenched I was, the better I felt. I had happy rain memories from my summer as a camp counselor in North Carolina, too, where evening downpours would beat on the tin cabin roof so hard that we'd have to shout over it to be heard reading out loud and saying goodnight to the girls. During my year of volunteering in Camden, New Jersey, I would take advantage of the rain to go puddle-jumping or just sit on the porch with a cup of tea and talk or think. On the Fourth of July that year, we went to a big outdoor concert without our rain gear and got dumped on for hours. We stayed through the fireworks, though, and then trekked the two miles home singing all the way, the rain never letting up.

This isn't to say that I never encountered the proverbial "rainy day" in a negative sense. At a summer day camp I attended around the age of 8 or 9, the end-of-session campout was the most-anticipated night of the summer. And, of course, it rained. I remember being shuffled out of our tents and into a picnic shelter after a long, wet, sleepless night, where the counselors held up soggy lost-and-found items: a lone sock, a pair of underwear, a Barbie doll. Another rough rain moment for me was during my semester abroad in Central America. Though I was there during the dry season, we did have a week or two of rain during which I first experienced the sensation of never really being totally warm or dry. In the region where I was living, buildings are not sealed off from the elements, there are no hot showers, and if you walk to work in the rain, you are wet all day. Rain in Juarez, Mexico, another place I've felt a connection to over the years, is rare and dangerous. Even the smallest amount of rain floods out streets and homes, and people are often killed. So my love for rain was always framed by a great respect: It was beautiful but powerful, and certainly outside of my control.

Little did I realize, however, that it's easy to find affection for rain when you are able to escape it. During the last 35 of our 44 days on the trail, I have not been so lucky, and I now have an entirely new understanding of what it means to be wet. On July 8th, the day we hiked Whitecap Mountain in Maine, my journal entry reads, "Rain! First experience . . . not too fun." Ha! What did I know??!

In the more than a month that has passed since I wrote those words, the freak weather system that has settled in has never granted us a full day without rain. We have been stranded twice due to high water making rivers impassable and once due to the risk of hypothermia in the freezing rain. Our clothes and shoes are never dry, and each morning we wake up and are forced to don them, cold and dank. Everything smells like mildew— pack, clothes, tent—and everything is caked in mud. Our packs don't just *feel* heavier—the sogginess of our belongings probably adds a good five pounds. We probably risk dehydration, because some days the thought of water just makes you rage. We often walk with frozen fingers and toes, and our constantly running noses must be blown on soaking wet handkerchiefs.

When we take off our shoes and socks at night, we (Laura especially) have been known to frighten small children with our "Klingon feet," eerily wrinkled and gray. Lizzie can't see out of her fogged glasses half the time, and there's never a dry ounce of fabric to be found to wipe them on. Stopping for a picnic lunch loses its charm when it means squeezing grape jelly onto a soggy bagel while sitting in a puddle.

Sometimes the AT is an ankle-deep stream, though it's true that that's better than the sections of waist-deep mud pits. On cold days, we can't stop or we'll freeze, and I've never been so desperate for a floor and four walls. Mountaintop views are a treat so rare that the slightest hint of a break in the clouds has everyone stopping, shouting for joy, and madly snapping pictures before the moment passes. Gore-tex is little more than a joke.

A caretaker at one campsite introduced us to the phrase, "No rain, no pain, no Maine," but even crossing the border into New Hampshire couldn't put an end to the deluge. Many others have told us, "Well it can't rain forever, right?" to which we respond with a shrug and return to wringing out our socks.

I can think of a number of explanations for the relentlessness of the rain we have faced. The first is Divine Punishment. Perhaps because of their religious skepticism, cold manners, or aggressive driving, God has decided to wipe out all of New England in a flood, and he forgot to instruct The Vermont Mafia on how to build an ark. Another possible explanation is Character Building. What doesn't kill us is said to make us stronger, so my comrades and I are being tested to the extreme. The only problem is that instead of making us tougher, this rain is softening up all our calluses and causing us to get blisters again. Of course another logical justification for 35 straight days of record precipitation is GLOBAL WARMING. This brings us full circle to Divine Punishment (we brought it upon ourselves), so I'm going to settle on some combination of all three reasons as ultimately responsible for the onslaught.

Now I am told that every cloud has a silver lining. Let me then attempt to mine the skies of western Maine and eastern New Hampshire for all they are worth. For one, we have re-learned the beauty of music. When we walked out of the rain into our first White Mountain Hut, Carter Notch, to smell baking pies and hear the banjo twangs of Alison Krauss, I felt comfort warm my soul as it hadn't in weeks. When we climbed through the window of the Wildcat Mountain Ski Patrol hut to escape the storm and wait out the night, thru-hikers Grizz and Earthworm serenaded us on the ukulele with tunes by Phish and Bob Marley. When we were visited on the trail by Lizzie's cousin Russ and aunt Jude, Jude's rendition of "Climb Every Mountain" from *The Sound of Music* made the thunder we were hearing sound pitifully weak. In addition to music, I have also learned to appreciate the silver linings of flexibility and faith. As if walking everywhere weren't enough, the rain has forced us to slow down even more. Doing less miles and not making planned destinations has—in spite of my initial groans—meant extra time with friends and family and more good stories to tell. Finally, every small blessing has taken on greater meaning— the sun, a patch of blue sky, a pair of dry socks, a four-walled structure, a warm drink. Hopefully I won't take them for granted anytime soon. I must admit that one thing can definitely be said for rain: It makes for memories. Soggy, saturated stories that run little risk of drying up.

Mahoosuc Moose

Tim A. Novak (Half Ass Expeditions)   **Northbound**
Mahoosuc Notch, ME
September 9, 1987

Maine started dishing out the thrills within a few miles of the border. Goose Eye Mountain provided some spectacular overlooks enhanced by the crystal clear mountain air. We stopped after hiking only 9 miles to Full Goose Shelter because we expected delays getting through Mahoosuc Notch. The next day was my birthday and I couldn't think of a better way to spend it than crawling through a pile of rocks!

Mark and I had heard all about the "Notch" and we were eager to experience the challenge. Just after the shelter, the Appalachian Trail dropped into a deep, rocky ravine. The woods were moist from a recent shower and the area had the feel of a rainforest. As we carefully stepped into the rocky cut, the air took on an unexpected chill. At the bottom of our descent into the Notch, we were struck by the massive jumble of huge boulders that was the Trail. I was snapping pictures faster than a caffeine-jacked photographer at a porn shoot as we clambered our way along that impossible path through the rocks. The going was slow but we didn't mind.

The Trail through the Notch was only a mile long and we savored every foot of the unique terrain. We had to take our packs off at times to get through some of the tighter spots At one point, Mark spied a note on a tree. "Dead moose 200 yards south." Sure enough, wedged in among the boulders was a large moose, preserved by the natural refrigeration of the deep, sunless Notch. It had apparently fallen from the cliffs above us. I understand a crew with a chainsaw later came and removed it. Nasty.

As if the obstacle course of the Notch wasn't enough, the climb up Mahoosuc Arm was a grind. The Trail was a sidewalk of exposed stone angled upward enough to require the hands at times, and today it was dangerously slick with rain. It took *all* day to hike the 5 miles to Speck Pond Shelter. And we were exhausted!

Mark and I stumbled into Speck Pond Shelter along with a ton of gomers coming in from the Grafton Notch direction. It was Labor Day weekend and it seemed the world was spending it at Speck Pond! There was an upside, though—lots of free food! Not only that, but I dined on fresh trout from the pond caught by a fisherman who hated fish. We ate well but had to spend the night answering a barrage of obligatory Appalachian Trail questions. Mahoosuc Notch and Speck Pond are truly beautiful spots and I understand why they are so popular.

Mark and I hoisted our packs the next morning for the walk into Grafton Notch. We stopped on an overlook for an early lunch of some gomer's leftover bagels. Our meal attracted the attention of one tenacious Canadian Jay. This bold bird climbed *inside* the food bag and swiped half a bagel. Within minutes I had it eating out of my hand.

Ups and Downs
in the Whites

Jennifer Ensworth (Thin Mint)   **Northbound**
Rangeley, ME
August 17, 2010

Hanover was a neat little town. It's the last town the trail passes directly through. It's also the home of Dartmouth college. The town was not exactly what I expected, but it had a certain charm to it. It was definitely a college town. I arrived in town on a Sunday and immediately I ran into Baltimore Jack (the trail legend who has hiked the trail eight-ish times). This was the fourth time I'd run into him. The second time I met him he had promised a place to crash in his home town of Hanover if he was in town. It turned out he was in town earlier than expected and his place was rented out. He himself was crashing with a friend. So instead of a place to stay I tried pumping him for info about the town. According to my book there really was no hostel and nowhere to take a shower or do laundry unless you stayed in a hotel and they started at $100 a night. He really didn't know too much. I asked him about some rumors I'd heard about a community center that has showers and laundry and a fraternity that lets you crash in their basement. Again he knew nothing. I was getting a bit frustrated when my friends arrived in town. I said goodbye to Baltimore Jack and we went to the Dartmouth Outing Club, which we were told would be helpful. It wasn't; there was a hiker board but it had no useful information.

So we went in search of the fraternity (I'd pumped a southbounder for info on Hanover, including this frat's address). The southbounder told me they take in hikers, but only four a night, and we were a group of six. We were hoping if nothing else they would let us shower. As luck would have it, they made an exception for us and let all six of us stay the night. So we stayed at the Phi Tau house (not Phi Kappa Tau). It's a coed fraternity and the cleanest fraternity house I'd ever been in. We stayed in their basement with the beer pong tables. I learned how to play the real "Beer Pong" which apparently was invented at Dartmouth. They play with paddles with no handles. It was a good night. The next day we went to the community center (closed on Sunday) and did laundry. It turns out Hanover is a pretty cool place, as long as you're not there on a Sunday

The Whites kicked my butt. They were tough. I knew they would be difficult, but I was not expecting some of the new challenges. Starting with the Whites, the mountains after a certain height are huge slabs of rock, so you might have trees and vegetation on both sides but the trail itself is just rock. The real challenge though is that they tend to always be wet and I do not do well on wet rocks. I didn't fall too many times, though this was mostly because my pace slowed so much. I did enjoy some of the whites, though—Mt. Washington, the Wildcats, and Mt Lafayette. For the most part I was not a fan. Along with the tough climbs there were the crowds, the lack of camping options, and the harsh weather above tree line.

I had my second worst day on the trail in the Whites. It was the day I came down Mt. Washington and it started out just fine. I'd stayed the night in a hut at 5,000 feet and climbed the $1^1/2$ miles to the top of Washington in the fog. The group and I hung out in the building up there for about an hour and by the time we were ready to leave the sky had cleared up. So we walked to the summit to get our photos taken. There were so many people there. We had to wait about five minutes to get one photo as a group. It should be noted that Mt. Washington is known for having the world's worst weather, so it is a pretty popular climb. There are also several ways to get there—hiking, car, and train. The real trouble started about thirty minutes after I left the summit. The weather turned shortly afterward and didn't get any better until later that evening. From Washington I had about 8 miles left of hiking above tree line in the rain and fog and it was miserable. The winds didn't let up for most of the day and by the time I was about a mile from the forest again I was praying for tree coverage.

Mt. Madison was one of the most uncomfortable climbs. The winds had to be 40 or 50 miles an hour and the trail up Madison was boulder climbing the whole way. Normally I enjoy boulder climbing, but the winds kept knocking me over. By the end of the day I was just worn out from the constant winds. Another reason the day sucked was I fell twice. The second fall was pretty bad on my knee. I had a moment immediately after the fall when I thought "This is it, it's over." Walking on my knee hurt for a while after that. Luckily what I thought was fluid in my knee has turned into a bruise so I think it's all right for now. That day I hiked 12 miles, but couldn't physically keep up with my group (the rest of them split up unintentionally that night as well into two groups of three).

I wound up night hiking for about an hour in search of a stealth camp sight. When I finally found a spot I started preparing dinner and realized I would have to eat dry that night. My stove igniter hadn't been working and I'd been borrowing lighters every night; since I was on my own that night I was out of luck.

The following day I was determined would be better and it was. I woke up really early at 6 A.M. because my stealth spot was a bit too close to the trail and I thought it would be best to be gone before anyone passed. I had a 2^1/$_2$-mile hike to Pinkham Notch and the trail to there was easy and pleasant. There was a camp store there and I bought a lighter and two cokes (because soda always puts me in a better mood). About a half mile past the road Greendog jumped out of the woods and scared the crap out of me. He was with Stitch and Landfill and they didn't know where the others were (somewhere ahead, so we thought). This is where I lost the group again. Stitch and Landfill went back to the notch to meet a friend and Greendog and I hiked on. I didn't see Greendog for several days afterward because I couldn't keep up, and Stitch and Landfill are still behind. The Whites get confusing because there are no good registers to leave messages and no good places to stay so no one knows where anyone is. Someone could pass your stealth campsite and you'd never know. I did the Wildcats that day and it was this really difficult but nice, steady climb. The weather was amazing and there were views of Mt. Washington all day.

The following day was another bad one. At this point I'm hiking on my own and it's the last day of the Whites. I made it to Gorham by 1:00, and got an easy hitch in. I bought a few snacks to get me to Andover, had lunch at Subway, and headed back to the trail. At this point I'd done 12 miles and wanted to do another 8 to try to catch the majority of the group (who were actually behind me, not ahead; only Greendog was ahead). I hiked another 2 miles and then started feeling sick. I thought it was the amount of soda I'd had so I kept of going. The uphills started getting pretty rough and I kept taking sitting breaks on the way up. About 1^1/$_2$ miles later I was in really rough shape. It'd taken me two hours to do that easy 1^1/$_2$ miles. I readjusted my plans, deciding to go to a campsite in another 1^1/$_2$ miles. It took me another two hours to get there. I also threw up five times. I was really weak by the time I arrived at camp. All the tent platforms were taken, but luckily

3 Bears was there and had room for another tent near him. I'm extremely grateful he was there that night. I tried to set up my tent but got lightheaded and had to lie down. He offered to set up my tent, then he got water for me, and took my food to the bear box. He also got water for me in the morning. I'm fairly certain I got food poisoning, as did two others from my group, which is why they are still behind me. They were fortunate enough to realize they were sick while in town and took a zero in Gorham.

I made it through the Whites, as expected, without having to pay anything. Two nights we found two really nice large stealth sites big enough for all seven of us. One night we did a work-for-stay at Lake of the Clouds hut (where we most likely all got food poisoning). I even talked my way into staying at a pay campsite when I was on my own. I asked him if he had a work-for-stay option. The only one he had was for in the morning and they make you do an hour of work. I was not interested in working in the morning when I could be hiking (and catching the group–which, of course, was actually behind me). I told him this and asked him if he knew of any stealth sites further on the trail. It was 7:30 or so at this point and he did what I was hoping he would do and said I could just stay there.

We were fortunate enough to have some pretty amazing trail magic in the Whites. Landfill, who is from New Hampshire, hooked us up. First one of his friends picked us up from a hostel just before the Whites and drove us to the trailhead without our packs. Our packs were dropped off at another friend's house so we could slackpack 16 miles. We were later picked up that evening and taken to Jim and Cathy's house. We were able to do laundry, shower, eat an amazing meal, and most of us had a bed to sleep in. The best part was they invited us back. So, three days later, after a horrible night of rain, we were picked up again at another road and taken back to Jim and Cathy's. They fed us again, we cleaned up, they took us to the store to resupply, and then they made us an offer we couldn't refuse— stay another day and zero. So we did, all seven of us. The five guys made themselves useful and did some heavy-lifting yardwork (Jim and Cathy retired in their 60s) and I helped with dinner. It was a real treat to cook again. I made my mom's marinara sauce and we had spaghetti which was great. I think the real highlight of the day was an out-of-the-blue experience. We went to a musical theater dress rehearsal. It was the most unique theatergoing experience I've had. The show was *The Mystery of Edwin Drood* and is an audience participation show. The cast needed an audience for their dress rehearsal and it was basically the nine of us and a handful of others. Normally, they charge for this, but when they found out we were thru-hikers they waived the charge. The show is based on an unfinished

Charles Dickens novel and in the end the audience gets to decide the "who dunnit." We all had a blast.

I'm happy to be out of the Whites and in Maine now. The first 30ish miles of Maine were a bit tough but seems to be getting easier. I saw my first moose in the Whites—the same way I saw my first bear, from a car. It was a little one and I got a video of it.

I'm currently in Rangeley, Maine. Right now my expected finish date is August 31st. 220ish miles left!

Of Shooting Stars, Falling Bodies, and Blueberries

Bruce Nichols (BirdMan)   **Southbound (Flip-flop)**
Stratton, ME

Dear Family and Friends,

I arrived this morning in Stratton, Maine, 187 miles south of Katahdin on the AT. So far northern New England is the land of R & R—that's rocks and roots. Walking south I've realized how new this landscape is. It wasn't all that long ago, geologically speaking, that the land that I have been walking over was covered by vast sheets of ice. And it is even more recently that the forests have returned. This is evidenced by the jumble of rocks and boulders that push up out of the thin covering of soil. Moss and roots thread their way around these old stones and the trail twists and turns in sometimes chaotic fashion around a myriad of obstacles. You need to pay a lot more attention to the walking. At times the trail might be a quater or half a mile of stepping from stone to stone. This is especally true on the steeper sections. I've had to climb a few rock slides already (many more to come). And yesterday I encountered my first 4,000-plus-foot mountain since southern Virginia (not counting Katahdin, which I climbed with a day pack). The east side of Avery Peak in the Bigelows was a steep, unrelenting climb of about 2,000 feet in a mile and a half on a hot and relatively wind-less day. I was infinitely happy when I finally arrived at the top, even though I still had 4 miles of rocky up-and-down ridge walking before I finally stopped at the beautiful little Horns Pond, nestled in a bowl high at the south end of the Bigelow range. But time to get back to the title.

Starting with **falling bodies.**

In which Bird Man (here more appropriately named Bird Brain) takes an unexpected Bird Bath.

A couple of days ago I walked down into Caratunk and waited for the "ferry" (a red canoe) to carry me across the Kennebeck river. The river was once crossed exclusively by fording but since a hydro plant upstream releases large quantities of water at unscheduled times, a ferry has been established for the saftey of hikers. Once across the river, the trail follows a beautiful stream called Pierce Pond Brook for about 3 miles to the pond, where there is a shelter. This stream is hallmarked by a number of beautiful waterfalls with lovely pools of clear green water just inviting a swim. I admired them longingly as I walked up toward the shelter, where I planned to take a break and perhaps a swim in the pond. (I've been able to swim almost every day of the walk so far.)

I finally came to a nice pool right by the trail and decided to at least splash a bit of water on my face and head, as I have done often on hot days both here in Maine and in the south. There was a convenient flat rock ledge at water level that dropped sharply into about 3 or 4 feet of water. I walked to the water's edge and bent over and splashed some cool water on my face. Then I lowered my head just a bit and rubbed some water into my hair. As I reached again for a second head splash I felt my center of gravity, which was rather percariously being maintained in favor of the rock, suddenly shift over to the water side of things. I must admit here that I had not taken off my pack, which was still buckled at the waist and definitely at this point working in favor of the brook. For just the briefest instant I thought I might be able to recover and just fall backwards but, alas, gravity and momentum are serious forces to be reckoned with. I'm not sure what it would have looked like to a casual spectator but my guess is that the resulting "fall" was somewhere between a face-plant and a belly flop.

I came up sputtering and was fairly quick to regain my feet and slog to shore, water streaming from my clothes, squishing out of my shoes, and draining off the outside of the pack. Fortunately, the drawstring at the top of the pack had barely escaped immersion and the contents remained dry (though I did not know this at the time). My main concern once I was back on the bank was for my camera, which rode in a waist belt and was completely submurged in the "dive." I had—just minutes before—put it into a ziplock bag, but I hadn't sealed the top. A bit of water had gotten into the bag and the camera was definitely malfunctioning. Once I'd gotten the dampness off the outside, I decided the best thing to do was to proceed as quickly as possible to the shelter and try to dry everyting out there. So—squish, squish, squish—I hot-wet-footed it down the trail, arriving at the shelter in about 15 minutes. I had already pulled the film (a new roll with only two exposures gone) from the camera to check the inside for dampness (just the tiniest little bit). So I popped open the back and took out the battery and laid the camera down in the sun and then proceeded to get out of socks and shoes and go through the contents of my pack to look for other damage/dampness. I was lucky that the sky was clear with low humidity and that there was a great sunny space in front of the shelter. It took about an hour and a half with repeated repositioning of the camera to get the dry heat into every part but the camera finally came back to life and seems to be working fine—as is the unexpected swimmer. The only casualty of the "big splash on the trail" was the little remote for the camera. This was not protected by a bag and was thoroughly soaked and as a result is nonfunctional. Sort of like my brain was when I decided to bend over that pool with my pack on.

On to **shooting stars.**

At the end of the same day I arrived at West Carry Pond, where I had a thoroughly enjoyable intentional swim. The Perseid Meteors have been going on for a few days and I decided that if I woke sometime after midnight I'd walk down to the lakeshore, which faced northeast, and sit out to watch a few falling stars. I did wake around one A.M. and, using my headlamp, found my way to a large, flat rock on the edge of the lake.

The night was very dark since the young waxing moon had set early. The stars were brilliant in the cool, clear air, with the milky way arching overhead and the big dipper sprawled out above the north horizon across the lake. The Pleiades were rising in the east, and Polaris hovered almost halfway up in the sky and due north. West Carry Pond is surrounded by low hills covered by fir and mixed hardwoods and I could just make out the dim silhouetts of the surrounding shores. An occasional bat—more a shadow than an actual body—flitted through my field of vision and vanished into the black. The air was exceptionally still and the sounds of frogs croaking across the pond a mile away floated out over the quiet surface of the water. And on that quiet surface another entire universe of stars lay spread before me.

I sat for a long time just wrapped up in this most wonderful silence. A few faint meteors cut the sky overhead. And then from some far corner of the pond, a loon raised its ethereal voice in a call of two pure, clear notes.

The sound reminded me a bit of a Native American flute, but it was even more liquid and captivating. In the natural hollow of those hills the call echoed slightly and reverberated. Just before it was gone completely there came a reply from some other quiet corner. And then back and forth, such a luxurious, luminous music, finally joined by more loons in their more charicteristic yodeling laughter. The whole of the pond filled with their music. And then, just as suddenly, it stopped but for the echos that hung over the water for a long moment.

I was dumbfounded, mesmeriszed, overwhelmed. I sat for some minutes, just feeling the effects of this concert for one. I finally rose and turned to go back to the shelter and my sleeping bag. As I stood, I noticed a rock near my feet and, on a whim, picked it up and threw it into the blackness of the night. I heard the splash, though I did not see where it hit. I could not see the spreading ripples either, but I watched in wonder as, one by one, the stars on the surface of the lake began to shimmer in an ever-widening dance of joy.

And finally—the **blueberries.**

I've always loved blueberries and, having spent a number of summers on the Maine Coast and also having a pick-your-own blueberry farm as a neighbor, consider myself something of an authority on the matter. On the trail between Monson and Caratunk, the AT passes over Moxie Bald Mountain and then Pleasant Mountain. In between the two it dips into a valley which is crossed by a power line that also happens to pass over the trail. Beneath that power line are the best blueberries in the world. I can make this statement with the authority of one who has been there and liberally partaken.

I spent the day passing and being passed by the Idaho 4—a wonderful family with kids ages 6 and 8 who walked all the way from Springer to Harpers Ferry and are flip-flopping back south as am I. I'd met them in Damascus and was happy to see them again. We arrived at the power lines at about the same time; they to lunch as planned and I, as it turned out, to enjoy a second lunch of the most delicious blueberries I've ever had. (Apologies to Terry Jones—my neighbor grower.) I sat down in a patch of large, perfectly ripe fruit growing in cluster of four to six berries and just kept filling my hand and pushing them into my mouth. In half an hour or so I ate what seemed like a quart (at least) and finally had to give up when I could eat no more (imagine that on the AT!).

Now, blueberries are good for you in serveral ways. They are fresh fruit, they're high in antioxidents, and they are also *great* fiber—I can attest to this also. So for at least one afternoon, Bird Man was a bit of a Blue Bird—a blue bird of blueberry happiness.

That's the skinny from Maine for now. Lots of R & R ahead as I enter the mountains of western Maine and then the White Mountains of New Hampshire. My next official stop for mail and resupply is Gorham, New Hampshire, probably in another ten days or so. Who knows, maybe there'll be a computer in Gorham I can get my feathers into.

Sunset on Bigelow Mountain

Philip Werner (Earlylite)   **Southbound (section)**
ME Hwy 27

I did a 75-mile section hike on the Maine Appalachian Trail last week and it was simply divine. The autumn color was in full glory and I had 50+ mile views for days on end. This hike had everything: drama, magic, danger, fear, thirst, fatigue, awe, and one singular moment of breathtaking elation that I don't think I'll forget for the rest of my life.

This time, I hiked from Monson, at the southern end of the 100-Mile Wilderness, to Maine Highway 27. In between, there are woods, mountains, lakes, moose, bear, mice, rocks, roots, mud, and not much else. This is true north country wilderness. In total, I saw about twenty-five people during my trip, mostly Appalachian Trail thru-hikers racing north, trying to reach Mt. Katahdin before Baxter State Park's closing date of October 15th.

Rain in Maine

Hiking in Maine is always complicated by a large amount of rainfall because there are so many river and stream crossings required along the Appalachian Trail. Naturally, there are few bridges, so the only way to get across these rivers and streams is by fording them, which can be dangerous in high water. Very dangerous.

When I hiked in the 100-Mile Wilderness last year, I experienced 6 inches of rainfall, and in a short period of time became somewhat of an expert on fording rivers.

In the days preceding this latest trip, central Maine received 4 inches of rain, causing widespread flooding and high river levels. This delayed a lot of thru-hikers across the state who had to camp beside rivers for days until water levels dropped enough to allow safe fording.

The number of river fords required on the Maine AT is unusually large in my experience, compared to hiking the AT in Connecticut, Massachusetts, Vermont, and New Hampshire. It's rare in those states to have a crossing that can't be done by jumping from rock to rock or wading through ankle-height water. I don't know what the AT is like down south, but Maine is off the charts when it comes to fords.

DAY 1: MAINE HIGHWAY 15 (NORTH OF MONSON) TO MOXIE BALD LEAN-TO (12.5 MILES + 5 MILES OF TRAIL MAGIC)

My friend hikezilla gave me a ride up to Monson, Maine, last Saturday. I met him at Grafton Notch in southern Maine early that morning and I was on the trailhead by 10:30 A.M. Monson is about a 7-hour drive north of Boston, about 3 hours north of the New Hampshire-Maine border, and in the middle of nowhere. You know you've reached nowhere when all of the stores you come across sell everything you could ever need, from fresh coffee to ladders, hunting ammunition, fishing waders, children's dolls and games, booze, over-the-counter medicines, deli meats, and subs.

The rain had cleared by the time I started hiking and the temperature was cool, in the low sixties in the sun, and cooler in the shade. I slipped into the woods, just south of the entrance to the 100-Mile Wilderness (which heads north) and started hauling through a kaleidoscope of autumn colors.

Truth be told, I don't think most thru-hikers hike the 3.5 miles of trail outside of Monson. Shaw's, the famous hiker hostel in town, runs a morning shuttle right to the 100-Mile Wilderness trailhead on Route 15, and it's easy to miss these miles unless you're an AT purist and make a point to hike every step from Georgie to Maine.

I hiked up and down rolling hills and past Lake Hebron, which borders the tiny town of Monson, passing a blue blaze trail and Shaw's sign nailed to a fallen tree. I was hiking at a pace of 2 miles per hour and continued straight to the banks of the East Piscataquis River, arriving after 3 hours.

Along the way, I met a section hiker who was just finishing up a short hike from Caratunk to Monson, some 3 days south. She told me that she had forded the Piscataquis, and the river had run up to her chest. Under normal conditions, this would be a knee-high crossing.

I was deflated and horrified. There was no way that was I going to do a chest-high ford. Even worse, she did it on the upstream side of a beaver dam. This is doubly dangerous because if you trap your foot in the dam, the water flowing downstream will pile up on you and push you underwater as you get tired and/or cold and hypothermic. A beaver dam is called a strainer in kayaking lingo and you always want to be on the downstream side of a strainer and never above it.

When I arrived at the river, I sat on the bank for a while just looking at the water level and considering my options. I could camp on the riverbank and wait for the level to drop, which would take a least one day; I could walk down to the highway and back up to the opposite bank—a 15-mile detour; or I could find another place to cross.

I scouted up and down the river for a while, looking for a better place to cross, and secondarily, for a nice campsite. In the end, I came back to the crossing and sat there for a while, looking at the beaver dam which people normally walk on to cross this river. One third of the dam had washed out completely and the river was pouring through here faster than the section that was overflowing the dam outright. None of this was good.

Trail Magic
It just so happens that there was a cooler of soft drinks placed on my side of the river bank, a common practice along the Appalachian Trail, where trail angels leave food and drinks for thru-hikers. Many of these trail angels are former thru-hikers themselves. This one was left by Strider, GA->ME '03.

About an hour later, Strider showed up, followed by his Dalmatian named BW, to pick up his cooler of soft drinks for the night. He saw me and we commiserated about the river level.

He agreed that a crossing was ill-advised, but he offered to drive me around the crossing and up the other side over Breakneck Ridge. This would leave me on the south side of the West Piscataquis, which is about 5 miles downstream of the East Branch where I was stuck, and was also running high. The river was running so high, in fact, that a Middle Branch had appeared between the two, requiring a third crossing!

It was an awfully kind suggestion and we took a ride around the rivers, down to the storeless town of Blanchard where Strider lives and back up the ridge along the unsigned gravel lumber and snowmobile roads that crisscross Maine. You either live here and know your way around, or you are lost.

This detour was the first section of the AT I had skipped, but under the circumstances, I viewed it as a justifiable pass. Thru-hilkers are technically only required to hike 2,000 miles of the 2,175-mile length of the Appalachian Trail, for this very reason.

Strider is a quiet guy but I was able to get some information out of him during our drive. He had hiked the AT a few years after retiring, after he had finished hiking the White Mountain 4,000-footers. I asked him why he'd hiked the AT, and he replied "I'm really not sure why," which is a pretty typical response, actually.

We arrived at the trail head after passing a half-dozen parties hunting grouse and said our goodbyes. It always makes me feel blessed when something like this happens to me, and deepens my commitment to pass trail magic on to others.

Gummie Bear

After parting with Strider and BW, I was still able to walk another 5 miles to the Moxie Bald Lean-to on Bald Mountain Pond before nightfall, putting in a respectable 12+ miles on such a short day. There I met another section hiker who was finishing up his thru-hike from the year before, when he'd hiked from Georgia to Hannover, New Hampshire on the Vermont–New Hampshire border.

His name was Gummie Bear and I came upon him wearing an unlikely sombrero, watching the sunset over the pond. I have no idea how he manages to keep the thing on his head while hiking! He told me a little about how the rain had delayed other thru-hikers up and down the trail, and I gave him the skinny on the Piscatiquis situation and his options. Basically, without a ride, he'd probably need to wait for the river to drop for a safe crossing.

The sun was setting rapidly, so I set up camp and then cooked dinner in the dark on the bank of the pond. Much to my alarm, the Piezo lighter on my Titanium Snow Peak Canister stove finally crapped out, and I found that I didn't have any matches in my emergency gear repair kit. It was cold each night of this trip, down to the twenties (Fahrenheit), and this was not good. Luckily, I also carry a Light My Fire magnesium fire steel, which I used for the first time ever on this trip. It worked great, and I don't think I'll ever carry matches to start a stove or fire again. This solution appears foolproof, and for only $8.

My menu for this trip was pretty simple, mirroring the multi-day menu I typically use on longer backpacking trips.
- For dinner: ramen noodles cooked in miso soup with a 1 oz shot of olive oil for extra calories and fat (700-1400 calories.)
- Breakfast: pound cake or other quick bread, smashed flat to save space, and packed in plastic bags (1000 calories.)
- 3 snacks per day consisting of Snickers, cookies, salami and crackers, Cliff bars, nuts, or licorice (1000-1500 calories.)

If you want more details about my backpacking menu preferences, they're discussed in the new camping cookbook *Food to Go*, coauthored by the popular Australian hiking bloggers Frank and Sue Wall, along with lots of good recipes from other backpackers.

After dinner, I hung my bear bag and fell asleep quickly to the sound of the wind blowing across the pond and in the trees. I was pitch-black out, so I thanked my lucky stars that I'd brought an Ursack and could just tie to to a tree instead of trying to throw a line in the dark.

DAY 2: MOXIE BALD LEAN-TO TO PLEASANT POND LEAN-TO (14 MILES)

The next morning I was up early, but lingered in my sleeping bag a bit longer than usual. The morning was chilly and I was almost a day ahead of schedule.

I broke camp by 9:00 A.M. and immediately started to climb Moxie Bald, a 2,600-ish-foot peak. Balds are mountains whose summits have been burned clear by fire. Conservation biologist Tom Wessels describes their ecology in the *The Granite Landscape*. If you've never read Tom's books, and you like to understand natural processes and ecology, they really are fantastic reads.

The previous day, Strider had told me that moose were common around Moxie Bald, but I didn't remember that until after I came upon a moose, right on the trail. At first, it looked like a really tall hiker, about 20 yards ahead of me, putting on a dark poncho. I was just about to call out "Are you a hiker or a bear?" when this enormous moose head swiveled back to eye me, and I realized this was a moose body. He (or maybe she) then made eye contact with me before it trotted off into the woods and vanished. Moose are my totem animal, so I viewed this as a good omen.

Moxie Bald was surprisingly challenging for such a short mountain. The trail quickly turned to rock-covered, with delicate alpine vegetation, and it became increasingly difficult to follow the scattered cairns. But the sun was out and the views were grand, so I took my time to take it all in. Moxie Bald is very exposed to the elements, so despite the sunshine, I put on my Rab Fleece to stay warm.

After summitting, I descended down the south side of the mountain to my first major stream crossing of the trip, across Baker Stream at Moxie Pond Road. This is a wide stream crossing, probably 30 yards across, situated just past a large beaver pond that is crossed by walking on top of the dam.

I reached the northern bank of Baker stream just as a thru-hiker named Ripple reached the southern side, and we waited to see who would go first. I got the impression that she was pretty unsure of herself, so I took the first plunge and found the water coming up to the bottom of my undershorts.

Gummie Bear had told me that this stream was waist-high when he'd crossed it the previous day, so it had dropped significantly overnight.

I picked my way across and made it to the other side without any issues, and then waited to make sure that Ripple got across safely. I noticed that we had different crossing styles, something I'd never considered before. She tried walking on top of the submerged rocks in the crossing, while I chose to stand on the streambed between the rocks because it's far less slippery. Maybe I just have more practice. It stuck me as significant, at the time.

After this crossing, I walked another 6.5 miles before stopping for the evening, passing another dozen thru-hikers and finally climbing Pleasant Pond Mountain. By now the day was waning and my feet were starting to get cold from trudging through big puddles and mud on the trail. Wearing trail runners this late in the year, even with wool socks, was uncomfortably cool in the early mornings and afternoons.

The views from the summit of Pleasant Pond Mountain were similarly spectacular to those from Moxie Bald. From there, it was a short steep descent to the Pleasant Pond Shelter, just off Pleasant Pond, where I again camped for the night under my tarp.

DAY 3: PLEASANT POND LEAN-TO TO WEST CARRY POND LEAN-TO (21 MILES)

I woke to my alarm at 5:00 A.M., well before the 6:30 sunrise, in order to get an early start. I needed to get to the Kennebec River, just over 6 miles away, between 9 A.M. and 11 A.M. in order to get a canoe ferry across it. This is a very dangerous river crossing that should only be done by boat, and the ferry ride is actually part of the official Appalachian Trail route.

I had breakfast and packed up, leaving at 6:35, when there was enough daylight to see by. Then I really turned up the pace, covering the 6.2 miles to the river bank by 9:00, where I met the Maine Guide who works for the Maine Appalachian Trail Club and ferries hikers across the river. I was first across for the day, and stood on the southern bank by 9:18.

As I headed up the trail on the opposite bank, I was passed by a dozen northbound thru-hikers racing to make the daily ferry window. Earlier in the season the ferry runs on an extended schedule, but this late in the year, its hours are very restricted. Miss it, and you have to wait till the next day to get across.

The walk south from the Kennebec is really a magnificent section of trail, passing miles of pristine waterfalls as the trail meanders through a dense forest alongside the Pierce Pond Stream. I made a mental note to return here in summer for some serious swimming and loafing.

After climbing a low ridge and passing Pierce Pond, the trail continues past several other lakes called East Carry Pond and then West Carry Pond. The "Carry" in their names signifies that they were used to shorten the distance required to portage trade goods into the region, by transporting them over water. Today, they are sparsely populated with private camps that are off the grid.

By now, the day was waning and I had covered 21 miles of trail. I decided to stop at the West Carry lean-to and sleep inside for a change because I had it to myself. Normally, I don't share lean-tos because I snore and I don't want to get kicked in the head when I'm asleep.

The West Carry Pond Shelter is by far the nicest shelter I'd seen so far on this hike, and is quite new in comparison to the others I'd passed. The site also has an extensive warren of good tenting spots, and is a popular shelter for thru-hikers because of good swimming in the lake in warmer weather.

I cooked up dinner and hung up my wet gear to dry before going to sleep at sundown and sleeping for a full 12 hours. It was great.

DAY 4: WEST CARRY POND LEAN-TO TO AVERY MEMORIAL CAMPSITE (14.5 MILES + 4,500 FEET ELEVATION GAIN)

After hiking 21 miles the previous day, my plan for day 4 was to take it easy and do a 12-mile hike to Safford Notch Campsite. The campsite is at a 2,000-foot col at the base of Mt. Bigelow, an awesome knife-edge 4,000-footer with a pair of summits at 4,088 feet and 4,145 feet. But things didn't work out quite as I had planned.

The two major peaks on Mt. Bigelow are in the center of a 17-mile ridge with secondary peaks to the north (Little Bigelow—about 3,100 feet) and south (The Horns—about 3,800 feet). The Appalachian Trail runs along the length of this ridge.

The pair of 4,000-foot peaks are named West Peak and Avery Peak. They are only 0.7 miles apart and separated by a 4,000-foot col called Bigelow Col. There are a series of tent platforms that form a campsite in the col, sheltered only by stunted trees growing just below tree line.

Hiking south, my plan was to climb Little Bigelow and camp at the Safford Campsite, 2,000 feet below the northern peak. I arrived as planned at 4:30 P.M., after an arduous climb over Little Bigelow, which is challenging in its own right.

Unfortunately, my plan for an easy day was thrown of course by an ill-behaved bear. The Safford Campsite, like other lower-elevation sites around the mountain, is having a bear problem this year, with bears stealing food and harassing hikers at night. This year's drought resulted in less naturally occurring bear food than normal, sparking this "aberrant" behavior.

I didn't want to deal with this issue at all, so I decided to climb to the top of Avery Peak (4,045 feet) and 1) try to summit before sundown at 6:30 and camp at the Bigelow Col campsite at 4,000 feet or 2) find a stealth site on the climb and spend the night there. The challenge was that I needed to climb 2,000 feet, in less than 2 miles, in under 2 hours, after hiking 12 miles beforehand.

It was a struggle, but I did make it to the summit and down to the Bigelow Col campsite just as the sun set. I was hyperventilating in fear when I made it to the top because I knew that I didn't have much time to traverse the narrow summit trail and get down to the campsite before I'd be surrounded by darkness.

Climbing Avery Peak this late in the day was a risky decision, but I did manage to pull it off—incredibly, since I was carrying a 20-plus-pound pack. Regardless, the feeling of summitting just as the sun was setting was an incredible personal triumph that I doubt I'll ever forget.

The sun set just as I made it to the campsite; I took the first tent platform I found and proceeded to pitch my Duomid on it for the night. Pitching a shaped tarp on a platform can be a challenge, but I carry a set of small eye-hooks for just this purpose and was able to get a good pitch soon after arriving.

I made dinner and took in the stars at 4,000 feet. The night sky was crystal clear and I saw more stars that night than I've ever seen on a hiking trip before.

DAY 5: AVERY MEMORIAL CAMPSITE TO MAINE HIGHWAY 27 (8 MILES)

Despite the elevation, I remained warm overnight, snuggled in my Western Mountaineering Ultralight 20-degree down bag and MLD Superlight Bivy Sack. I had also packed chemical warmers (Grabbers or Hotties) just in case I did get cold on this trip, but I didn't need them.

The following morning, the sky was overcast and it was clear that we were due for more rain. I intended to be in Stratton, Maine, before this happened, where I planned to rest overnight in a motel, resupply, and decide whether I wanted to hike for another week. I was starting to feel my IT band acting up and questioned whether I'd be able to comfortably finish the remaining 75 miles to Grafton Notch, where my car was parked.

Lying in my sleeping bag, I looked up the number of the motel in the pages of the AT guide that I'd brought along, and reserved a room for the night using my cell phone. Then I packed up, had a short breakfast, and proceeded to climb the West Peak of Mt. Bigelow and the Horns, and hike the remaining 8 miles to Maine Highway 27.

Ascending the higher West Peak of Bigelow was an easy climb from the col, but I still needed to climb another sub-peak called South Horn before I could descend from the Bigelow Ridge to Highway 27.

After South Horn, the AT drops down to Horn Pond (3,250 ft), where there are two lean-tos, a summer caretaker, and a large number of tent pads. It's a nice place to camp, especially if you're hiking north along the AT. I refilled my water bladder here before descending the next 4 miles to Highway 27, passing through a pleasant wooded area with some bog cross-ings before reaching the highway. From there I had an easy hitch into Stratton, Maine, just 8 miles to the east.

After a night's rest in Stratton, it was pretty clear that I was going to have IT band issues if I kept hiking south for another 75 miles, so I arranged for a shuttle back to my car, parked in Grafton Notch. I had had an awesome hike as it was, and plan to do the remaining section next spring.

A Ride in the Gravy Boat

Tim A. Novak (Half Ass Expeditions) **Northbound**
Kennebec River, ME
September 29, 1987

It had been so long since Mark and I had seen the sun, we'd started to speak of it as if it were legend. The air was relentlessly waterlogged and the low foliage soaked us as we brushed against it. The fall colors were at their peak and the damp washed a hard-shell hue on the yellows and reds. Mark and I spooked a mama moose and her baby that morning and I failed to reach my camera in time to get a picture. It was an uplifting sight on an otherwise dismal day.

I think we were getting used to the wet, as we hiked a fast 11 miles to Piazza Rock Shelter despite the weather. Knowing there was a dry spot waiting for us helped quicken our pace. Lido Bandito, California Dave, and Figgy Newton were already in residence, filling the shelter with the familiar smell of trail food, stove fuel, camp farts, and body odor. It was the welcome stench of a dry night under the roof of our temporary Appalachian Trail home. Mark and I settled into the shelter and added a few of our own odors. The topic of the evening was the weather. It was unanimous . . . we were all sick of the rain.

Maine is beautiful when the sun is shining on it. We woke to a heavy fog shrouding the shelter, but the sun burned it off before we had hiked our first mile. Our spirits lifted with the mist as we hiked through the colorful forest. We enjoyed a lively ascent of Saddleback but the clouds hung at the

135

summit and the icy wind sent us on our way. A bit later, atop Saddleback Jr., the views were awesome. The clouds were thick in the low spots and it felt as if we were much higher than the 3,900 feet stated on our map. We absorbed the commanding vista for quite a while, taking time to mentally catalog all the impossible colors of the foliage. We were dizzy with optical overload when we stumbled into Poplar Ridge Shelter a few miles later.

The second highest peak in Maine is off the Trail but we made the detour. Near the summit, Sugarloaf Mountain hosted a large gondola lodge to serve the skiers in the winter. Now it was empty and we moved right in for the night. The winds howled and a piece of plywood covering a window hole fell inside with a startling crash. Later that evening, our camp stove caught fire and I feared an explosion of compressed Coleman fuel. After a few panicky moments, the blaze went out and soon we were settled in for the night.

Instead of taking the AT into Stratton, Mark and I decided to walk down the ski slope to the road into town. After a knee-damaging descent off Sugarloaf Ski Area, we poured onto the main drag and hitched toward the food. We arrived in Stratton, got a room at the Widow's Walk ($10.00 for a room and breakfast!), and proceeded to feed. We retrieved our mail drop, repacked, and prepared for more magnificent Maine.

In the morning we stuck out our thumbs and hitched back to the Trail under the rare Maine sunshine. It was a great day for hiking and we were about to climb into one of our favorite hunks of wilderness!

Mark and I ascended the peaks of Bigelow enthusiastically. It seemed every turn in the trail opened up onto an overlook and great big eyefuls of brilliant autumn color. The surrounding terrain was splotched with many huge lakes. The ski slopes on the scarred face of Sugarloaf were the view south across the valley all day. We ran into Highlander and Mike on the way up. We all lingered a bit on a particularly nice ledge then hiked on to Avery Memorial Shelter for the night. Aside from a resident rabbit and one of those annoying Canadian Jays, Mark and I had the place to ourselves.

The following morning we got up at dawn and started the climb of Avery Peak with the sun still close to the eastern horizon. The views from the summit were outstanding. Great masses of clouds seemed to be eating the landscape far below. The valleys were stuffed with cottony wisps, and tendrils of mist followed the river cuts on the mountainsides. The camera worked overtime as I struggled to capture the Kodak moment. But no film could really represent the vista from the peak that morning.

The Kennebec River was the largest river we had to cross without a bridge. The stories of peril and even death as a result of wading across haunted the Trail registers. Not to worry . . . the wonderful state of Maine provided a "ferry service" for Appalachian Trail hikers. It was a low-budget program featuring a scruffy guy and his trusty canoe. According to rumours, he would be there twice a day to perform his service. A bunch of hikers hung out patiently on the south bank to wait.

While we waited we saw a motor boat being plopped into the water. We were all sure this was our ferry. As we watched, the gomer standing in the boat pulled hard on the motor's starter cord. Like a graceful figure skater he spun about and the boat launched out from under him. He hit the water on his back and the boat drifted downstream. We watched as he clumsily retrieved the boat, suggesting to each other that we wade across. Just as we were contemplating our swim to the other side, we saw our ferryman with his canoe waving from the north bank. He was a likable man who loved his cushy state job. As he paddled us across he told us his reason for wearing a life jacket was "to keep from drowning in the gravy."

We spent that evening with Cookie Monster, Peter, and Judy at Pleasant Pond Lean-to just outside Caratunk, Maine. The following day we walked 13 more miles through yet another day of rain. Mark and I were soaked through to the skin by the time we poured into Moxie Bald Shelter. We were 16 miles shy of Monson, the last trail town and the gateway to the 100-Mile Wilderness. We had less than 130 miles of Appalachian Trail left to walk!

Wet Boots in the 100-Mile Wilderness

Philip Werner (Earlylite)   **Northbound (section)**
Spectacle Pond to South End of Nahmakanta Lake, ME

I started a 9-day trip on the 100-Mile Wilderness section of the Appalachian Trail last Saturday, but ended up getting shuttled out after 6 days and 74 miles due to a knee/quadriceps overuse injury. Staying out for 6 days on a solo really pushed me mentally and physically in ways that I've never experienced on a shorter section hikes. Uncomfortably so, even. Yes, it's a bummer that I didn't finish, but as a section hiker, I can always pick up where I left off, another day.

DAY 1: SPECTACLE POND TO LONG POND STREAM LEAN-TO (15 MILES)

I started a little late on Saturday by my standards, only getting to the trail at 8:20 A.M. But I had decided to be mellow and enjoy the breakfast experience at Shaw's Lodging, which was fantastic: great food and great company. Sometimes, online, you can get the feeling that thru-hikers don't respect section hikers, but there I was sitting with northbound thru-hikers, southbounders who had just started their hikes, and other section hikers, chatting away like best friends. It felt really comfortable and goes to show that there aren't any barriers between hikers when they all get together in person.

When I had finished my breakfast, I was eager to bolt, and to their credit, Shaw's shuttled me to the trail by myself, even though there were easily a dozen or so other thru-hikers and section hikers who planned to start that day. Before I left, Dawn, the innkeeper, gave me a short, serious talk about some of the dangers ahead. She warned me that the rock in Maine is made out of slate and is very slippery when wet. In addition, she warned me about fording rivers, something I'd never done, and the fact that the streams were all running higher than normal from the 2 inches of rain we received the day before. Finally, she explained that they'd be happy to come pick me up if I got into trouble and I was near one of the logging roads that cross the trail, and that the best cell reception, if any, would be from mountain tops.

A lot of people will tell you that the 100-Mile Wilderness is not a true wilderness anymore, and there's a certain amount of truth to that, but it's still not a good place to have a bad fall, break a leg, or have a serious medical emergency. While I was there, I witnessed one serious rescue operation and heard about a second. While there are gravel logging roads that bisect the trail every 10 to 20 miles, cell phone reception is very poor and it could easily be over 24 hours before a SAR team could reach you. Even after that, the terrain is so difficult that extraction would likely have to be a manual one over a very rough trail. I was carrying a Personal Locator Beacon at the request of my wife, so as long as I was conscious to operate it, I knew I'd have a better chance at getting help in a worst-case scenario than someone relying just on a cell phone.

Regardless, I was eager to get some miles under my belt and when I was dropped off at the trailhead, I set off hiking at about about 1.5 miles an hour in light rain. I was feeling good, but my Mariposa Plus backpack was stuffed to capacity with 9 days of dehydrated food and weighed a bit over 36 pounds, including fuel and 2 liters of water. That's about 12 or 13 more pounds than I'd normally carry on a 3-day section hike and I was looking forward to eating down the load as the days progressed.

The trail was pretty muddy, but I managed to keep my boots dry for two hours. After that I fell off an unanchored log bridge into a muddy bog up to my waist! That was special and pretty much set the tone for the next 6 days. Having hiked the Long Trail in Vermont last year, I thought that the Green Kingdom had the worst mud in New England, but I can assure you that Maine's mud is far worse and there's a lot more of it, despite the excellent trail maintenance work performed by the Maine Appalachian Trail Club and the Maine Conservation Corps.

Swearing at my stupidity—I could have hiked around the mud pit—I continued on to a beautiful waterfall called Little Wilson Falls, which is the tallest waterfall on the entire 2,172-mile Appalachian Trail at over 100 feet high. It drops into a narrow slate canyon that is about 300 yards long and it was really cranking from the recent rain.

The trail parallels the falls down the south side of the canyon to Little Wilson Stream, which has to be forded. This was the first ford I'd ever done with a backpack, so I was a little nervous, but luckily there were two thru-hikers on the other side of the stream that I knew from breakfast and they just waved me over. The crossing was pretty easy, even with the extra water in the stream, and it came up to my knees, completely soaking my socks and leather boots. I had brought some camp sandals which I had hoped would work for river crossings like this, but they weren't going to provide me with the support I needed to cross rocky rivers full of waves and holes, and by the second day, I gave them away to some kids so I wouldn't have to carry the extra 11 ounces.

Once across, I took off my boots and squeezed the water out of them. Then I took off each outer wool sock and sock liner and did the same to them. I repeated this ritual for the rest of the trip each time I had to ford a river. This made my leather boots a lot lighter, but they never dried out completely after that and there were times when I felt like I was wearing cinder blocks. I am now convinced that I have to give up leather boots for this type of terrain.

After that I continued across rolling woodland, fording another three streams, two of which had ropes for hikers to hold onto. While emotionally comforting, these lines were not well placed in my opinion, making the crossings more hazardous than necessary.

Despite the crossings and the delays caused by wringing out my socks, I made pretty good time the rest of the day, passing two shelters and arriving at the third, the Long Pond Stream Lean-to, by 7:15 P.M. My thru-hiker buddies were in the lean-to, which looked a little scuzzy, and there was a son and father camped out in a tent who I would become good friends with in the following days. I scouted around and ended up picking a tent site above the shelter. It wasn't perfect, but I wanted some privacy and peace and quiet my first night out.

Next, I cycled through my normal make-camp routine. I hung my two heavy bear bags, almost breaking my jaw in the process when the rock came back at me after snagging on a branch and hit me in the face. I thought I tasted some blood, but there was no way I was going to quit a hike that I had been planning for seven months, so I just took a big Ibuprofen pill and hoped the pain would go away. Next I filtered water, pitched my tent, cooked dinner, changed into my sleeping clothes, recorded a audio diary entry, and went to sleep.

. . . until five minutes later, when eleven young hikers and their counselors came in from the dark with headlights from Barren Mountain and proceeded to make camp directly behind me! They went to sleep two hours later and I finally got to sleep at about 11 P.M., a little pissed off, you might say. They only shut up when it started to rain.

DAY 2: LONG POND STREAM LEAN-TO TO CHAIRBACK GAP LEAN-TO (11 MILES)

After the Long Pond Stream Lean-to, the Appalachian Trail continues north over the Barren Chairback Mountain Range, a series of five named peaks that are all under 3,000 feet in elevation. I'd been told that some of the best views in the Wilderness are along this range, but the trail was completely socked in by clouds both of the days that I was climbing it, with intermittent showers during the day and torrential rain at night.

After leaving the previous night's tent site, I had a long climb, just under 2,000 feet, to the summit of Barren Mountain (2,670 feet), where there are remains of an old fire tower. Surprisingly, tree line on the range starts at about 2,300 feet, quite low by New Hampshire standards, where it usually starts about 2,000 feet higher up. The other peaks in the range include Fourth Mountain (2,383 feet), Third Mountain (2,061 feet), Columbus Mountain (2,326 feet), and Chairback Mountain (2,219 feet).

During the day, I became friends with John and Matt, the father and son duo that had been camping at Long Pond Stream the night before. We had been passing each other during our respective rest stops all day until we both got to Monument Cliffs on Third Mountain and formal introductions were made.

They were from northern Rhode Island and had some good section hiking experience on the Continental Divide Trail and in the Rockies. We would end up hiking from shelter to shelter for the next four days at the same pace and I got to know them a little better each day. John is a carpenter in his mid-fifties and Matt goes to college down in Virginia. I came to admire and even envy their companionship during the hike: It gets lonely hiking solo on a long trip and it would have been nice to have a partner along to break the tedium.

At about 5 P.M., I arrived at the Chairback Gap Lean-to, which had a really odd layout. The shelter is at the top of a steep hill that descends about 150 feet to a tannic bog which is the shelter's water supply and produced nasty, brownish water. The tent sites are about 75 yards above the shelter on another steeply eroded slope.

The shelter was full of men with dogs that liked to growl at other hikers, so I gave them a wide berth and ended up camping above the shelter area in a half-stealth location that was blissfully flat and protected from any more late-night arrivals. I had a satisfying pasta dinner and crashed before 8 P.M., sleeping once again through another night of torrential rain.

DAY 3: CHAIRBACK GAP LEAN-TO TO SYDNEY TAPPAN CAMPSITE (12 MILES)

I woke up the next morning at 5 A.M., but it was thundering and raining hard so I went back to sleep for another 90 minutes, breaking camp at 8 A.M.. With all the rain we'd been having at night, my sleeping bag was beginning to get soaked from internal condensation in the tarp tent. I wasn't that concerned about warmth even though it is a down bag, but I knew that it was getting heavier to carry and I needed to dry it out somewhere.

The fog and intermittent rain continued as I walked over slate ledge to Chairback Mountain, the final peak in the range. Chairback is so named because the north side is a near-vertical drop down onto a slide of giant bolders, followed by a steep walk through woods to the West Pleasant River (above) and another ford. This was the longest ford of my trip and the water was running high, coming up to my waist during the crossing.

After wringing out my socks, I continued along the Gulf Hagas Stream, which is a wondrously beautiful series of cascades, waterfalls, and rapids bordering Gulf Hagas, a unique slate canyon that extends northwest from the trail. By now the weather had started to clear up a bit and the sun was finally coming out when I caught up to John and Matt and we ran into a rescue that had already been underway for three hours.

A young girl, about thirteen years old, had suffered anaphylactic shock as the result of a bee sting and was slowly being evacuated down the trail afer being jabbed with an EpiPen. Someone had hiked out to call the state police and they had her conscious and upright supported by two other rescuers. This was a camp group and the counsellors, young by my standards, were clearly trained in wilderness medicine and doing a good job.

We were briefed by one of the rescuers and when it was clear that we weren't needed for assistance, we continued on to the base of Gulf Hagas Mountain (2,683 feet). This was a 750-foot climb, but I was treated to stone stairs that had been built by a trail maintenance crew almost all the way up. They had done a beautiful job. We ended up meeting two crews out doing trail maintenance on White Cap Mountain that weekend.

After you summit Gulf Hagas Mountain, you still have a walk of about a mile to get to the campsite, mainly through blueberry bushes and jewelweed. I flew through this bit but could hear thunder behind me from an indeterminate location. I've been in situations like this before, so I was relieved when I made it to the Sydney Tappan Campsite without being zapped by a lightening bolt.

A crew from the Maine Conservation Corps had already set up an elaborate base camp by the time I arrived, taking up most of the good tent sites, hanging a mess tent, and setting up a multi-rope bear hang just outside of camp. They were a very friendly group of young college-aged kids who were doing trail work all summer and were on site for a few days to build more water bars.

I set up my tent and hung my sleeping bag out to dry in the sun and soon my gear soon dried out. What a relief! By then, John and Matt had arrived and we cooked up some dinner. But just as it we started to eat, it started to thunder loudly and it got eerily dark outside. I hurriedly finished my meal and hung my bear bags just before a huge thunderstorm hit us. It was really coming down, so we all got into our tents and went to sleep.

DAY 4: SYDNEY TAPPAN CAMPSITE TO EAST BRANCH LEAN-TO (9.5 MILES)

I woke up to showers the next morning, but I got my gear packed away and headed out by 8 A.M. My goal was to summit White Cap Mountain (3,654 feet), the highest peak in this section and the lesser peaks before it before descending to the East Branch Lean-to and trying to dry out my gear again.

I was mad at myself for not packing a bug canopy or bug bivy on this trip so that I could sleep in the shelters during the heavy rains. It was a toss-up really, because the shelters up to this point had been very unappealing to sleep in, but a tarp, sleeping bag bivy, and head net/bug canopy combo might have been a more flexible system under the conditions. I still can't decide if the Squall 2 was the right shelter to have brought along on this trip.

Always the optimist, I was hoping the the weather would clear a bit so I could get some views off White Cap. Given my pace, I had pretty much abandoned the chance of hiking into Baxter State Park and climbing Katahdin by this point within the 9 days I had available and I was just aiming to finish the 100-Mile Wilderness section, ending at Abol Bridge.

Before, climbing White Cap, I had to ascend two other wooded, viewless peaks called West Peak (3,178 feet) and Hay Mountain (3,244 feet). West Peak was a 750-foot climb in less than a mile from the campsite, but it was a easy climb due to another beautifully built series of stone steps. Next, I continued up the more gradual dome of Hay Mountain, where I started passing a number of southbound hikers. They reported clear skies and great views on top of White Cap but insane mud to the north in the flat lakes region of the trail.

After another two hours of hiking, I summitted White Cap. The views were good. Many of the surrounding peaks were cloaked in a lingering haze but I could make out Katahdin about 75 miles to the north. John and Matt were just packing up when I arrived. They were covered in flies, so I didn't linger. I quickly changed out of the rain pants, which I had been wearing for the past three days, into my normal long hiking pants, bolted down some food, and continued on.

After a short descent through scrub and krumholz, I reached tree line again and met another trail crew building stairs. It looked like hard, wet work, but they made it look easy: hoisting rocks from the slopes in the surrounding woods and moving them to the trail on a complex system of pulley lines. After waiting for a safe moment to pass, I continued down White Cap, and was soon walking though a beautiful section of trail starting at the Logan Brook Lean-to and continuing to the East Branch Lean-to, where I stopped early for the evening, arriving around 2:30 P.M.

I had hours to kill before dark, but the first order of business was to dry out my gear again, repair my bear bag system, which had been giving me problems all trip, and investigate a problem that I was having with my water filter.

This wasn't my usual bear bag system, but a second one that I threw together at the last moment to carry my food for days five through nine of my trip. The chief difference between the two is the cord. For the new system, I grabbed some thin spectralite line that I had sitting in my cordage drawer at home. Although strong, it was so thin and slippery that I was having a hard time pulling it without it cutting into my hands and even burning them if I lost my grip. To make it more usable, I devised a different way of using it by cutting it in two and tying one half to the bear bag and the other to a tree, and then connecting the two using an extra mini-biner. This worked out much better for the rest of the trip.

After that I went down to the stream to wash out my clothes and diagnose a problem that had just cropped up with my First Need water filter. The problem first started the evening before on Gulf Hagas Mountain. The First Need has a two-stage filtration system: A prefilter for filtering out particulates is attached by a long hose to the main filter, responsible for filtering out organisms and toxic chemicals. I knew from experience that if you tear a hole in the hose the productivity of each pump goes down and the pump makes a sucking sound, which it was doing now. I couldn't find a hole by visual inspection so I cut the hose in half, reattached the ends, and found the hose with the hole on the second try.

I thought that this had fixed the problem, but the next time I used the pump the problem was back and I was forced to use my backup chlorine dioxide tablets to purify my water. By pure luck, I did find a workaround which was to keep the filter parallel to the ground when pumping. I suspect that a simple backwash will fix this problem, but I'm glad that I always carry a few days of Micropur chlorine dioxide tablets in my gear repair kit as a fallback.

After that I relaxed, recorded another audio journal entry, and hung out in my tent watching my feet deprune. They were still holding up well despite the mileage and wet boots. After a while, I ate a huge pasta dinner with genoa salami and was asleep by 6:30 P.M.

DAY 5: EAST BRANCH LEAN-TO TO ANTLERS CAMPSITE (15.5 MILES)

With the mountains finally behind me, I knew that I'd be able to pick up my pace and crank out some more mileage. So I broke camp by 6:30 A.M. the next day and headed out. John and Matt were just packing up as I left—they had also stopped at this campsite to dry out the night before. But, of course, we had another river to ford just outside of camp and it came up to my waist.

After wringing out my socks, I continued on, climbing a small hill called Little Boardman Mountain (approximately 2,000 feet) before heading down to the Crawford Pond area and starting the section of the trail that would continue at an elevation of about 600 feet for the next 60 miles, past numerous ponds and lakes, all the way to Abol bridge.

The weather was great and I was finally able to turn on some speed over the level ground despite my wet boots. I made it to Cooper Brook Falls Lean-to, a distance of 8 miles, in just over four hours, and stopped for lunch shortly afterwards. My right knee had started to hurt, badly enough that I was limping, so I took a 600 mg ibuprofen before I hiked another 8 miles to the Antler's Campsite, arriving exactly at 3 P.M. The trail up to this point had just been beautiful all day. I had been walking parallel to Cooper Brook for much of the way on an easy trail cushioned by pine needles and largely void of mud, roots, and rocks.

I sat down outside the entrance to Antlers, the location of a former fishing camp on Lower Jo-Mary Lake, and had a snack. I could have easily continued on to the next shelter or beyond and cranked out a 20+ mile day. But my limp had worsened and I decided to call it an early day and have a bath in the lake instead.

No one else was at this campsite that whole evening, so I had the place to myself, and I picked an incredible tent site surrounded on three sides by the lake on an isthmus surrounded by red pine trees. People hike in the 100-Mile Wilderness to camp at pristine locations like this.

I set up camp as usual, and then went skinny dipping and had a good wash with some Dr. Bronner's liquid peppermint soap which I had brought along for just such an occasion. This was my first wash in five days and I felt refreshed to be clean again. I rinsed out some clothes and then lazed around, barely clad, until dinner, watching the ducks and goslings paddle around the lake and trying to predict the weather from the clouds. There had been a brisk breeze all day that had blown out the big cumulus clouds and I was hopeful that I'd have fine weather the next day.

I made a great dinner that night and went to sleep early again but woke up at about 8 P.M. The sun hadn't set yet, but I could see that the lake was fogged over completely. I suspected rain, so I dropped the front vestibule of my tent and went back to sleep until morning.

DAY 6: ANTLERS CAMPSITE TO WOOD RD/SOUTH END OF NAHMAKANTA LAKE (11 MILES)

I didn't hear a thing after that until I woke up the next morning, but it had apparently rained at least 2 more inches overnight and it was still pouring when I woke up. I lingered in the tent as long as I could stand it and then packed up all my wet gear again and set off.

My limp had grown worse overnight and I was not doing so hot when I arrived at what should have been a small stream crossing. The rain had turned it into a roaring river full of downed trees and other hazards. I scouted for a better crossing and even considered sitting there for half a day to let the water level drop. In the end, I figured out a way across, but I was unsettled by the experience. John and Matt had not camped at Antlers the previous night and must have continued on to the next lean-to. I knew that there was no one behind me for at least a day to pick up the pieces if I got into trouble.

After the stream crossing, I started climbing Potaywadjo Ridge. I have been down the knee and quadriceps injury road too many times and was really questioning my ability to last another three days with the pain. I knew that this would be my best chance to get cell phone reception for the next 24 hours, as the ridge was at an elevation of close to 1,000 feet, and decided to try to call Shaw's for an extraction. It seemed like the best option to prevent any further damage to my knee. As I sit here (several days later) writing, I now know that it was the right decision. I can barely climb stairs at the moment.

Just then I met a southbounder named Jared, who was in far worse shape than me. He had a bum ankle and knee and was limping very slowly down the trail. I told him that I was going to try to call Shaw's and that he was welcome to join me if I could get a shuttle out. Amazingly, I did manage to reach Shaw's, although my connection was dropped four times during the call. I arranged a shuttle pickup 8 miles to the north at the southern end of Nahmakanta Lake for 5 P.M., giving us 8 hours to get there. We actually made it there by 1 P.M., which is amazing considering the trail conditions that we encountered along the way.

The trail conditions were horrendous. Every tiny stream we came to was in flash flood mode and hazardous to cross. I can't even remember how many we had to ford. The trail looked a lot like the swamps of the Everglades in Florida or the bayous of Louisiana, minus the alligators, of course. Many sections of the of the trail were completely underwater and after a while I just gave up trying to stay dry and sloshed through the calf-deep mud.

We arrived at our destination several hours early for our pickup but our adventure was far from over. It turned out that the gravel logging road we were waiting on had been washed out farther downhill the previous evening by the rain. We found this out from the assistant director of a girls' camp located at the end of the road, who told us that they couldn't get any trucks out for food pickups or trip shuttles. We couldn't get any cell reception from where we were to call Shaw's to warn them or to make alternate plans, so I suggested we just sit tight and see if they could make it through as planned anyway. There were several places where we could still camp out if we needed to wait another day for a pickup, and neither Jared or I had what I considered a critical injury.

In the end, Gary arrived from Shaw's at 5:05 P.M., having driven through the washout in a Honda CRV to get to us. We were so happy to see him. The washout was pretty impressive when we came to it on the way out and I could see how trucks or vans with longer beds would have a hard time getting through it. It was about 3 feet deep and maybe 5 feet wide. Gary got out and moved some rocks when we got there and then drove right though it. It was great. We arrived at Shaw's by 7 P.M. and headed south from there toward Boston in my car.

Jared and I had by this time become good friends. He's a great guy and I hope to meet up with him again. He lives in Manchester, New Hampshire, so I offered to take him down to Portsmouth, New Hampshire, on my way back to Boston, so he could get picked up by a family member. He was seven days into a southbound thru-hike when he got injured, so he decided to bag his entire trip. I tried to talk him out of this, but he had decided to go in the spur of the moment after getting laid off from work, despite having little prior backpacking experience. I think he was glad that he did a one-week trip, and learned a lot, but decided that he needed to ease into the thru-hiking experience a little more gradually. I really wish him well.

Editor's Note: Philip completed the final twenty-six miles of the 100-Mile Wilderness in 2011.

Katahdin

Maria Dickinson (EKG)
Katahdin, ME

Northbound (Flip-flop)

I seem to recall the Vermont Mafia saying they heard the phrase "No Rain, No Pain, No Maine" last summer. The trend continues.

I started out from Gorham with my friend Dan to hike the last section of my thru-hike to discover a cache of trail magic courtesy of Sunbeam (SOBO '08). I greatly appreciated the Little Debbies and Dr. Pop! After that, however, we had lots of fog, two days of rain, and lots of mud, as Dan gained his trail legs, endured the Mahoosuc Notch, and learned everything about backpacking from how to poop in the woods to how to purify water. He was a great sport as my mood fluctuated, and I was sorry to say good-bye when our different hiking paces drew us apart. (It turns out that my miles are the miles of a fiendish finishing thru-hiker and are a bit ambitious for a first-time backpacker.)

At a lovely hostel called The Cabin I met Panama Red and Jolly Rancher, who invited me to join them in a 26-mile slack pack the next day, to be picked up by Bob O'Brian, who owns the Gull Pond Lodge in Rangeley, Maine. Slack packing is where you have somebody take your full pack for the day, while you do big miles with a day pack. It is a really sweet way to make miles, but it can be expensive because you have to pay for your host's road mileage there and back. Thankfully, it is cheaper when you split the fare, as I did with Panama and J.R.

We actually slacked the next three days, once again with Bob, then two days with Susan from the Stratton Motel. It was really nice to get some of the more rainy Maine days out of the way while sleeping indoors every night. Dan even caught up with me in Stratton, on our second day there, and I saw him the next day as we were going over Saddleback Mountain. Saddleback is a beautiful ridge above treeline, where, at the summit, you can see both Mt. Washington and Mt. Katahdin on a clear day. I met Dan on the summit that last day amid the beauty of sun, wind, mountain views, and clouds and we made our adieus as he went on to hike on his own and I went on with Panama and J.R. to the finish. It was a beautiful though somewhat sad moment.

After our final slack packing day, it was time to get to Monson, home of Shaw's hostel. We did it in three days, staying at Pierce Pond and Moxie Bald Brook shelters the two nights. Pierce Pond has a reputation on the AT for being the most beautiful shelter location, and this is not without reason. The shelter sits on the pond's edge amid a beautiful pine forest. We got in early and watched the sunset on July 9th, Panama's birthday and the day the rainy weather in Maine broke. The next morning I went to Harrison's camp, a camp mostly for anglers and day hikers. But since it's just on the other side of the pond from the AT shelter, he provides amazing "patriotic" pancakes (apples, blueberries, and raspberries) for breakfast for hikers. I decided it was worth the detour and was treated to perhaps the most delicious homemade pancakes I've ever eaten. Though I must admit, on the trail as a whole, I had many a pancake and most were the best I've ever eaten…

We then had a string of nine days of sunshine, maintaining the weather to our glorious finish!

We got in to Monson on the third day, stayed at Shaw's hostel (also famous on the trail) and ate tasty barbeque and enjoyed the usual town gamut of laundry, showers, comfy beds, and good company. The most wonderful thing about Shaw's, however, is their all-you-can-eat breakfast, complete with eggs, bacon, sausage, and pancakes. They ask you what number of everything you'd like, and keep pumping out the dishes until you say "no more." Wow. That was amazing. Plus coffee and OJ. Mmmm-mmm.

That day, however, we began the 100-Mile Wilderness. A word about this well-known trail section: The signs warn you to take ten days (minimum) worth of food and supplies once you enter, because there are no (paved) roads and it is some of Maine's thickest and wildest woods. Most Southbounders are happy to get it done in 10 days or maybe 9 or 8. Same with section and day hikers. We, however, originally planned to do it in 6, since there are some good flat bits on the northern end. We planned roughly 20ish-mile days for each day.

The first day we did 15, and were happy to meet a recently finished '09 NOBO hiker (Splinter) who had come back to the trail to do magic. He greeted me at Long Pond shelter with a six-pack each of PBR and Long trail ale. I was happy to meet him indeed. Panama and J.R. soon joined us and completed the party. That was an excellent finish to our first day in the "Wilderness."

In the "wilderness" you also can get cell phone reception on any hill or mountain above 2,000 feet.

Next day we did 21 miles to Carl A. Newhall Lean-to, and on arriving (after seeing a moose about 10 feet in front of me on the trail!!!!), I discovered three section hiker men and two SoBos already in the six-person shelter. Panama, J.R., and I had all mailed our tents home to shed weight for the final stretch, so perhaps the first few words out of my mouth after greeting them were "I don't have a tent and there are two guys behind me who don't either. Do any of you have tents?" Amazingly (amidst much groaning and whining) the two SoBos got their stuff together and got out of the shelter, heading toward the tent sites nearby. I felt pretty bad, but they were amazingly compliant about it. When my boys arrived, they were tickled pink that I had cleared out the shelter for them and even a little surprised at the SoBoers' amicability. When I asked them what they would have done if the SoBos hadn't gotten out, they said, "Kept walking." Mind you, this would have been 4 more miles up and over Whitecap Mountain after 8 P.M. I was glad the SoBoers didn't consider this option!

That night Panama was mischevious. He was talking about pulling some 30-mile days and finishing the wilderness in the next two days instead of three or four. J.R. and I (the more planning-minded of the three) were dismissive at first, but Panama's amazing gift of gab and convincing abilities were in high form so we finally said that if he got up the next morning at 4:30 to hike 30 miles, we'd do it with him.

Sure enough, as 4:30 A.M. dawned gray and still, we silently packed our things, gobbled some granola bars, and headed over Whitecap. I was full of adrenaline, excitement, and a sense of rebellion as we hiked our knees sore that day. With 11 miles to go at 3 P.M. at our afternoon snack stop, I was nervous that the next shelter would be full as well and we would arrive too late and not be as lucky as the night before. There was a small possibility of hiking a few extra miles and getting a ferry across a lake to White House Landing, an inn and restaurant about a mile off the trail, but in order to achieve that, we would have to make it there before sundown, which I was estimating would be at 7 o'clock or so. Anyway, with all of these worries buzzing around in my brain, I decided to try and hike the rest at 3 mph, so I booked it.

I got in to an excellently empty Potaywadjo Springs Shelter at 6:20 P.M., followed soon after by the boys at 6:30. We had booked it and finished a glorious, beautiful day through some very easy, very flat trail (much of which was open, pine-floored trail with a gorgeous brook or lake on one side—"wilderness" indeed!).

But the craziness wasn't over. Panama proposed a 33-mile day for the morrow, in order to complete the Wilderness and arrive at Abol Bridge, a campground 15 miles from Mt. Katahdin. J.R. and I didn't argue when the alarm sounded next morning at 4 A.M. and we were off again, coasting over flat, muddy trail with many a lake or brook on one side and a few little hills on the way.

One of those hills, Nesuntabunt, went up to 2,000-some feet, so I (naturally) pulled out my cell phone to try and figure out a ride out of Baxter State Park. I called Cousin Jim with five bars of reception, (we had exchanged messages for a few days before, so he knew that I was now thinking of summiting on the 18th), and told him I could summit either Friday the 17th or Saturday the 18th, depending on weather. I had new flexibility since we had made such crazy miles. He told me to let him know when I knew and that not only could they come pick me up at Baxter state park and take me to their place in Tamworth, but that Cousin Jim would drive me to Middlebury the next day. I was thrilled to have security about returning to civilization.

Then I hiked 24 more miles.

At the 5 miles-to-go mark after Rainbow ridge (which had a stunningly breathtaking view of Mt. Katahdin, sunny and clear of cloud cover), we stopped briefly at a shelter. Panama and J.R. were already there when I arrived. I crashed on the ground, feet throbbing, knees aching, and brain turned to mush from the tedium of it all. The boys were in high spirits, thanks to "5 Hour Energy" and "Gu"—they were into taking diet supplements to aid their hiking ability (Read: lots of B vitamins and Taurine—ICK!!)—but I was dragging. That is, until I ate a snickers bar and took some good old vitamin I (ibuprofen). Then I was plucky as new and ready to "get 'er done"!

We emerged from the "Wilderness" and crossed Abol bridge, to see none other than Panama's dad and brother-in-law in a van with a huge tub of pasta salad, leftover chicken, a dozen boiled eggs, champagne, and all sorts of goodies. Huzzah! What a finish! We gobbled everything in sight and settled in for the night at the Pines campground on the lake's edge, exhausted and content.

The next beautiful sunny day we did the easy 9 or so miles to Katahdin Springs campground, and rested at the ranger station there, chatting with the ranger and somewhat confused about what to do with ourselves since we had a complete half day of nothing to do. We hung around, ate lunch, made a fire, and chatted as we waited for Panama's crew to arrive with promised pizzas and beer for dinner. They soon came (amidst the beginning of a downpour) and we feasted on three pie-tins of spaghetti, three large pizzas, and an 18-pack, sitting inside our nice dry and warm shelters. Mmmmm, sooo lovely!

The next day, Friday, Panama, his crew, and I planned to summit because we were really ready and because the weather was forecasted to be better than Saturday. J.R. was waiting for his family who would arrive to hike Saturday, so he took a zero in Millinocket (a town 20 miles away). The day dawned cool and foggy, but without rain. I ate my last breakfast and packed my day pack for the day. (The ranger station at Katahdin allows you to leave your full pack and take day packs they have there for that purpose.)

I started up the trail at 6:30 A.M., happy to be hiking "Big K," finishing what has been such an amazing journey. It was surreal and hard to believe, I must admit. Here I was, a mere 5 miles and 4,000 feet away from the completion of a hike that began last August with the Vermont Mafia at Franconia Notch, New Hampshire. I was full of happy anticipation and eager to move.

What a hike, what a hike! I think I can say without room for much doubt that it was my favorite part of the trail. No mud, hardly any tricky roots, and after the first mile or two, mostly rounded granite rocks and large-grain sand. The Katahdin stream and waterfall accompanied me for the first hour, clear, freezing, and jolly as it poured off the mountain. I then came to a section where my poles became useless as I grappled up rocks, an occasional rebar aiding my path. I passed two groups of students as I began to make it above the clouds, and the morning sun shone on the white-gray rocks. The trees became fewer and fewer as I moved above treeline and made it onto the "tableland," a flat section on the AT approach trail to Katahdin that runs along the ridge until the final incline. What a view! The air was cool and crisp, with a breeze blowing fog across the ridge occasionally, followed by brilliant sunlight and mountain views. My eyes remained ever forward, scanning the steep horizon for a now very familiar sign post amid the blowing fog and blinding sun.

And then, after I had almost resigned myself to wait longer than I'd thought: There it was! A crowd of people stood atop jagged rocks looking out at the view, but only one thing held my gaze: the Katahdin sign, standing so seemingly unaware of its much-photographed glory. I increased my pace unconsciously until my hand finally grazed the well-weathered wood, the white painted letters nearly completely rubbed off. I couldn't believe that here within my grasp was the so-much-sought sign that adorns many a thru-hiker thank you and Christmas card, poster, and t-shirt.

YES!!!!

I raised my arms in exaltation and joy and stretched to the sky—a silent Huzzah! in my head, and for a brief moment, the world was all light, joy, and strength!

Then my mind came back to the mountain itself, and realized that the other people on the mountain had no idea. Okay, maybe they had some idea, because they too had climbed to this glorious peak, but they didn't know the quarter of the trail. From eavesdropping, I learned they didn't even know what the AT was. It was a group of kids from the city out in the "wild" to do a character-building thing. I set myself on a rock perch and just took in the view and tried to absorb the gravity of the moment. My silence and beaming inner joy seemed right, and I was content to have this nearly private celebration in which to bask as I enjoyed the top of The Mountain.

After a bit, I did a little hike out onto the Knife Edge, another approach trail to Mt. K that is an aptly named glacier-carved stretch of ridge where a false step means serious injury and there are steep fall-offs on either side. At a certain point, though, (where the trail went down, and returning would mean more up), I turned back to Mt. K to see if Panama and his family had made it up yet. As I came back, I saw him in his familiar hat and red beard, beige shirt and blue shorts striding up the trail. I let out a victorious whoop and he responded in kind as he came to the sign, kissed it, and gave me a smiling high-five.

YAY!!!!

We ate lunch together with his dad and brother-in-law and enjoyed the continuing clearing up of the sky as the sun burned the fog away. After many a photo of creative poses on and around the Katahdin sign, I decided to head back down the way I'd come. I had started at the base at 6:30 and summitted at 9:30, and I left the top at 12 or so and made it to the bottom at 2:50 P.M. I picked up my 2,000-miler application at the ranger station, picked up my full pack, and relaxed, waiting for Panama and his family, who were giving me a ride to Millinocket.

What a tremendous journey it has been! My heart swells with gratitude and joy for the adventure we've experienced—but thank God it's finally complete! I am now officially an AT flip-flop hiker: SOBO Franconia Notch, NH, August 2008, to Springer Mountain, GA, December 2008, and NOBO Franconia Notch, NH, June 2009, to Mt. Katahdin, ME, July 2009.

Greetings and blessings to all of you and thanks for following me on this final bit of the Vermont Mafia's A.T. Adventure.

The End of a Journey

Preston Lee Mitchell
Home
September 8, 2009

The AT journey has been complete for a week now and I think I'm ready for a reflection. Since finishing, I've been sitting in chairs, sleeping in beds, and eating in restaurants—all novelties for me at the moment. Reading everyone's blog and facebook comments has been really enjoyable and I want to thank everyone who followed along and offered their words of encouragement. I've spoken to some of you on the phone and a general theme of conversation has been "Okay, so you walked 2,000 miles and lived (mostly) outdoors; what did you learn?"

The first thing I learned is that the AT is the most ineffecient and ridiculous way to travel from Georgia to Maine. Seriously—I Google-mapped driving directions between Amicalola State Park, Georgia, and Baxter State Park, Maine, and driving distance is only 1,000 miles, less than half the distance of the AT. Not to mention all the ascents and descents on the trail! But of course no one undertakes this journey to simply get from point A to point B.

I learned that I will never ever tire of Snickers bars. I tried many energy bars but ultimately Snickers won out. Best boost of energy. Most calories per weight. Tastiest. I think I was up to one or two king-size bars a day by the end of the trip.

Kidding aside, what I really learned is how lucky we are that the Appalachian Trail exists. It's pretty amazing that in the span of the last century the Appalachian range has transformed from a polluted, over-logged, and economically depressed area into a beautifully protected and managed forest. It's a "green tunnel" through the heavily developed eastern U.S. Many people criticize the National Forest and Park Service, but ultimately I was walking through older and healthier forests in 2009 than the politicians and volunteers who came together to create the trail over 70 years ago. We are a lucky nation—and I'm part of a lucky generation—to be able to take advantage of the conservation and park movement of not just the Appalachian Trail but of all our national and state parks.

I don't think I learned anything new about myself. I didn't have any kind of philisophical breakthrough, nor was I expecting to. I enjoyed my time living in the woods and out of a pack, but I'm also pretty excited to move back into a walkable, exciting city. The AT was something I thought I would enjoy and now I've checked it off the "bucket list."

I learned that it was physically hard, but mentally harder than I ever expected. And I thought I was prepared mentally. When considering whether they will make it all the way to Maine, many thru-hikers have the saying "I'll hike until I'm not having fun anymore." Well I'm here to say if you actually abide by this philosophy, you're never going to make it to Maine! Don't get me wrong, I had a blast on the AT, but just like normal life, there were days that just plain sucked. It may have rained like hell all day, I might have have tripped on every rock and root one day, or maybe I woke up and just didn't want to hike. But I simply had to because if I took a day off I would run out of food before I made it to the next town. I also missed people who I couldn't see while hiking and sometimes couldn't call when there wasn't cell coverage. But ultimately, the fun days far outweighed the bad ones and I would do it all again. The beautiful vistas, the sense of setting and reaching small goals every day, and the incredible people who I shared joy and hardship with along the way made it all worthwhile.

Throughout the trip, day hikers and people in trail towns would notice my beard, tattered hiking clothes, and perhaps my general lack-of-shower stench, and ask me "Are you a thru-hiker?" Concerned about jinxing my trip, instead of saying "Yes," I always returned the question with "I'm trying to be." I even said this when people were giving me premature congratulations on the last 50 miles of the trail.

For most thru-hikers, the defining "end moment" is when they finally see the Katahdin summit, take the last steps of the trail, and snap celebratory photos at the terminus sign. The defining end moment for me was after the celebratory activities. I was climbing down the mountain when I passed a day hiker who predictably asked "Are you a thru-hiker?"

I responded "Yes. I am."

About the Contributors

Amanda Redpath (Veggie)
redpathATadventure.wordpress.com
   Since hiking the AT, Amanda graduated from Syracuse University, finished the Adirondack 46ers, and participated in the NOLS New Zealand Semester. Her next goal is to hike the PCT. She blogs about her latest adventures at thebackpackerchronicles.wordpress.com.

Amanda Schlenker/Jarrod and Becca Schlenker (Hansel and Gretel)
jabeccawalk.blogspot.com
   Amanda Schlenker served as chronicler for her brother and sister, Jarrod (trail name: Hansel) and Rebecca (Gretel), who hiked the AT to raise money for the Multiple Sclerosis Association of America. Jarrod is currently pursuing a law degree at Catholic university and working on Capitol Hill; Rebecca is pursuing a law degree at Quinnipiac University. Amanda is a pediatric occupational therapist in New York state.

Bruce Nichols (BirdMan)
www.shinealight.com/write/index.htm
   Bruce Nichols lives in Shelton, Connecticut, where he works on projects for several nonprofit groups, including Friends of Peace Pilgrim, the Siddhartha School Project, and the Shelton Land Conservatrion Trust. Since his 2002 AT hike, Bruce has continued his long-distance hiking with walks of the Camino de Santiago in Spain, the Long Trail in Vermont (twice), the John Muir Trail in the Sierra Nevada, a walk from Nagasaki to Hiroshima in Japan, and a 700-mile walk and kayak journey from his home in Connecticut to Canada and back. His next walking project is the newly designated New England National Scenic Trail from Connecticut to New Hampshire.

Corwin Neuse (Major Chafage)

walkingwithchafage.blogspot.com

Corwin Neuse is a freelance adventurer, screenwriter, novelist, and world-renowned lover. As a student at Tisch School of the Arts at New York University, he studied Dramatic Writing, perfect preparation for a life of shiftless misadventure. Corwin currently lives in New Haven with his girlfriend and their cat.

Deb Lauman (Ramkitten)

www.debralauman.com

Deb Lauman completed her thru-hike in 2000. Today she lives in Flagstaff, Arizona, and is a freelance writer and the author of *I. Joseph Kellerman* and *A Picket Fence in Pawpaw*. In addition to her online trail journals, she blogs about her experiences as a search and rescue volunteer at http://debssarstories.blogspot.com.

Devon Parish (Flamebo)

5millionsteps.wordpress.com

Devon Parish and her fellow members of the Vermont Mafia (Beef, EKG, Default, D-Wreck, and Bearwalker) completed their southbound thru-hike in 2008. Flamebo is currently working for an environmental non-profit in Boston, Massachusetts, where a good hike is never more than a few hours away. Despite now living with four walls and a roof over her head, she still never takes being warm and dry for granted.

Elaine Rockett (Second Stage)

trailjournals.com

Alas, Elaine Rockett was unable to complete her anticipated thru-hike in 2010. Happily, however, she plans another attempt in 2012. She'll be posting updates on trailjournals.com.

Elizabeth Zane (Beef)

5millionsteps.wordpress.com

Elizabeth Zane completed her southbound thru-hike in 2008 in the excellent company of the Vermont Mafia (Default, Flamebo, EKG, D-Wreck, and Bearwalker). Since finishing the trail she has tackled her next adventure—medical school—in the wilds of Syracuse, New York.

Francis Tapon
francistapon.com

Francis Tapon is the author of *Hike Your Own Hike: 7 Life Lessons from Backpacking Across America,* and *The Hidden Europe: What Eastern Europeans Can Teach Us,* which will be released in April 2012. After completing the Appalachian Trail and the Pacific Crest Trail, he became the first person to do a round-trip on the Continental Divide Trail. His goal in life is to visit every country on the planet (so far he's been to eighty) and share the experience with others.

Jennifer Ensworth (Thin Mint)
trailjournals.com

Jennifer Ensworth successfully completed her thru-hike on August 31, 2010, summiting Mt. Katahdin on a beautiful day with an amazing group of friends. Since then, she has been doing freelance work casting films and television in New York City and Nashville, Tennessee.

John Bryant Baker (Sunrise)
bakersthruhike.blogspot.com; www.johnbryantbaker.com

John Bryant Baker works as a whitewater rafting guide and carpenter, with his favorite river being the Gauley in West Virginia and his favorite project being the 1989 transit bus that he and his wife call home. Since their thru-hike in 2010, whether on the river or on the trail, they have continued to experience the awe of nature and the empowerment of adventure.

John Bitner (Churchill)
trailjournals.com (journal listed under "My American Dream")

John Bitner is from Audubon, New Jersey; he graduated from Rutgers University and worked at Cooper University Hospital in the ICU. Since finishing the trail he moved to Tampa, Florida, where he works in the emergency department at Tampa General Hospital and is co-authoring a book about the Appalacian trail with another hiker.

John Pugh (Johnny Swank)
sourcetosea.net

John has hiked the Appalachian Trail and paddled the Mississippi River; his future plans include hiking the Pacific Crest Trail and mountain-biking the Continental Divide Trail. He earned a master's degree in Recreation and Sport Science from Ohio University in 2003. John is from the one-stoplight town of Climax, NC.

Julia Tyler (No Promises)

juliashike.blogspot.com

Julia Tyler grew up in Wisconsin and studied religion at Macalester College in Minnesota. She now lives in Ventura, California, where she works as the Director of Religious Education at the Unitarian Universalist Church of Ventura. When she's not at work, she reads, writes songs, and continues to dream big. She hopes to complete the southern half of the Appalachian Trail someday.

Karelyn Kressler (Little Dipper)

karriesappalachiantrail.blogspot.com

Karelyn Kressler completed her southbound thru-hike of the Appalachian Trail in November 2009. The following year, Karelyn and seven friends canoed the Mississippi River from the headwaters in Minnesota to New Orleans, raising funds for relief efforts in Haiti. Now she is living on a sustainable farm in North Carolina and hopes to take on the Pacific Crest Trail next.

Maria Dickinson (EKG)

5millionsteps.wordpress.com

Maria Dickinson finished her hike of the AT in the summer of 2009, and returned home to Albuquerque, New Mexico, to start taking prerequisite classes for physical therapy school. She also attended St. John's College and began working part-time as an office assistant and a tutor for kids with autism. She is now applying for physical therapy school and enjoying playing rugby and day hiking in the beautiful Sandia Mountains.

Nicole Green (Ichiban)

greenattrek.blogspot.com

Nicole Green, a teacher from Texas, was a first-time long-distance hiker. She plans to go back to school for a second Master's degree in higher education.

Peter J. Barr (Whippersnap)

peterontheat.com

Peter J. Barr became fascinated with the AT on a family vacation to the Great Smoky Mountains National Park when he was eight years old. Ten years later, he returned to the Smokies to hike on the AT for the first time; his visit to the Shuckstack lookout tower during that hike changed the direction of his life, leading him toward a career in land conservation. His thru-hike in 2010 raised funds for the restoration of the deteriorated Shuckstack tower. Peter has hiked all 900 miles of trails in the Smokies as well as climbing the highest 200 peaks in the southeast, and has written two books: *Hiking North Carolina's Lookout Towers* and *Hiking the Southeast's Highest Peaks*. Peter is the Trails Coordinator at Carolina Mountain Land Conservancy in Hendersonville, North Carolina, where he lives with his wife Allison.

Philip Werner (Earlylite)

sectionhiker.com

Philip Werner writes about backpacking and hiking full time for several online publications, in addition to his blog. When he's not section hiking the AT, he volunteers as a Long Trail Mentor for the Green Mountain Club and maintains a hiking trail at the base of Mt. Washington in New Hampshire.

Preston Lee Mitchell

apptrail.wordpress.com

Preston Mitchell was inspired to hike the AT after growing up near the trail in North Carolina. He thru-hiked in 2009 and has since been living in Washington, DC, with his wife and newborn baby boy. His dream is to hike the AT with his son.

Stuart Skinner (Tintin)

trailjournals.com

Stuart Skinner was awarded a fellowship from the Winston Churchill Memorial Trust to hike the AT to promote the mental health benefits of outdoor activity. He has written a series of columns on the mental health benefits of hiking for the outdoor magazine *Country Walking*. Since finishing the trail, he qualified as a bushcraft instructor and set up a charity called Jurassic Wilderness Acadmey, which runs bushcraft expeditions and conservation camps for young people at risk of social exclusion. Stuart lives in Weymouth, England.

Tim A. Novak (Half Ass Expeditions)

www.blistersdicegame.com/trail1.html

Tim Novak finished the Appalachian Trail in 1987 and went back to hike 700 more miles of the Trail in 1989. Tim continues to hike sections in New England, prefering to hike the Maine sections in the winter months. When Tim is not hiking on the AT, he can be found speeding down hills on his Street Luge.

Towns

mikesathike.blogspot.com

Towns is twenty-five and lives in Atlanta, Georgia, with his wonderful girlfriend and a very lovable three-year-old Weimaraner, Bella. He is currently trying to figure out what he would like to accomplish next and continuing to enjoy the simple pleasures of life like being able to shower every day and step indoors during a thunderstorm.